DEVELOPING INNER

STRENGTH

CHARLES
STANLEY

OLIVER
NELSON

THOMAS NELSON PUBLISHERS
Nashville

Published in Nashville, Tennessee, by Thomas Nelson, Inc.

Scripture references are from the NEW KING JAMES VERSION of the Bible. Copyright © 1979, 1980, 1982, Thomas Nelson, Inc., Publishers.

ISBN 0-7852-7284-4

Printed in the United States of America
1 2 3 4 5 6 7 HDC 04 03 02 01 00 99 98

CONTENTS

RECEIVING GOD'S GIFT OF INNER STRENGTH

One of the most wonderful statements that Jesus ever made was one that He made about Himself and what He desires to impart to us:

> *The Spirit of the LORD is upon Me,*
> *Because He has anointed Me*
> *To preach the gospel to the poor;*
> *He has sent Me to heal the brokenhearted,*
> *To proclaim liberty to the captives*
> *And recovery of sight to the blind,*
> *To set at liberty those who are oppressed. (Luke 4:18)*

Jesus came to this earth not only to take care of our sin problem and to make it possible for us to experience forgiveness and eternal life, He came to make us whole from the inside out.

With wholeness comes emotional, mental, and spiritual *strength*.

The Holy Spirit is God's ongoing gift to us that we might become more and more like Jesus and experience what He purchased for us on the cross in an ever deepening, ever more potent way.

No matter who we are today, we are "poor" in some way. We each lack something or are a little weaker in one area of our emotional makeup than in other areas. No person is 100 percent strong in all areas of his or her life at all times. Just as we are healthier physically on some days more than others, and at some periods in our lives we are physically fit than at other periods, so we go through periods when we experience a weakness or a "hit" in our emotions.

When those times of emotional weakness come, we generally experience emotional pain. If we deal with our emotional pain as soon as it arises, receiving God's help and healing for the injury we have suffered, this pain is generally temporary. At other times, however, the emotional pain lingers. We may not deal with it, hoping it will go away or heal itself. We may not know *how* to deal with the pain, and thus, continue to struggle on without relief. We may not believe that we *should* deal with the pain, thinking perhaps that pain is inevitable and a normal part of every person's life.

If you are experiencing emotional pain today, my word to you is threefold:

1. Time will not heal your pain, but Jesus Christ can and will heal you in your emotions if you turn to Him and receive the strength He offers to you.

2. The Bible presents to you God's ways for dealing with emotional pain; you must learn what the Bible says and apply God's truth to your life.

3. God desires for you to live in emotional freedom and strength, unshackled by emotional weakness or inner pain.

The results of an ongoing, lingering emotional pain—a pain that goes unaddressed and unhealed—can be devastating to a person and to a family. Lingering or pervasive emotional weakness saps a person's energy, drains away creativity, diverts the person's motivation and enthusiasm for life, impacts his or her relationships, and, if left unhealed, can cause serious damage to the person's physical health and to overall effectiveness as a witness for Christ in this world. My friend, *none* of these conditions are God's desire for you! Rather, God desires that you be filled with a vitality and enthusiasm for life, be creative in every area of talent and skill that God has placed in your life, have healthy and vibrant relationships, experience a maximum amount of physical health in your life, and be both a productive and an effective witness to the gospel of Jesus Christ.

Let me ask you several questions today:

- Are you lonely?
- Do you feel restless and frustrated?
- Is anxiety eating away at your joy?
- Do you feel burned out . . . insecure . . . broken . . . as if you are a failure?

These conditions are all symptoms of emotional wounds that weaken us and make us more vulnerable not only to manipulation and injury by other people, but also to attacks in the spiritual realm. These are the very symptoms that Jesus came to heal and to strengthen when He said that He came to

- heal the brokenhearted,
- proclaim liberty to the captives,
- bring sight to the blind,
- and set at liberty those who are oppressed.

Emotional pain and weakness cause us to feel dejected, "bound up" on the inside, blind to the goodness of God, and imprisoned in our own darkness. Jesus came to set us free and to make us whole; He came to impart to us a deep, abiding, and consistent strength, and then to develop us so that we move to *greater and even greater strength in Him.*

Are you willing to receive the strength that the Lord desires to impart to you?

Our Part in the Process

Jesus is the Savior, the Healer, the Deliverer, the One who makes us whole. There is a twofold role, however, that we are required to play in bringing about a healing of our emotions and in receiving God's strength.

1. *We must be willing to set down our emotional baggage. Emotional baggage* is a term that refers to old feelings, thought patterns, and past experiences that continue to traumatize a person every time they are triggered or recalled. Some people have become so accustomed to carrying heavy emotional baggage that they can't imagine life without that burden. They are so familiar with emotional pain that they can't imagine life without pain. In fact, the thought of "letting go" of something in their past, or of a hurt they have nursed through the years, is threatening to them.

In some cases, a person may feel that he is opening himself up to increased vulnerability or greater accountability. Both may be true, but what is *not* true is that greater vulnerability or accountability automatically leads to greater or renewed pain. Jesus can be present in any situation to comfort, love, and nurture us when we make ourselves vulnerable to Him and open up our lives to receive the fullness of His love and forgiveness. Jesus is present whenever we face up to our sin or seek to make amends and grow spiritually in our lives; He helps us become accountable to ourselves and others, always in a framework of love and forgiveness.

There is no benefit in continuing to carry emotional burdens. There is no good reason for hanging on to what slows you down, keeps you from being vibrantly alive and strong, or stops you from experiencing the fullness of life that God has prepared for you. On the other hand, there is every *good* reason to set down your emotional baggage at the foot of the cross and to walk forward in your life with a new freedom to your step!

Today is a great day for coming to the Lord and saying, "Lord Jesus, I am at the end of my ability to heal my own emotions. I cannot make myself strong. I lay down my emotional burdens, pain, and weakness at Your feet, and with Your help I resolve never to pick them up again."

2. *We must invite the Lord to do His work in our lives.* The Holy Spirit will not overstep the boundaries of your own will. God will not invade your life and strip away from you your painful memories or heal your withered emotions unless you *ask* Him to do this work in you. Today is a great day for asking the Lord Jesus to take from your heart the emotional load you are carrying, to heal your emotional wounds, to bind up your emotional pain, and to set you free from emotional bondage . . . and to impart to you His strength. Invite Him to begin a healing work within you: "Lord Jesus, I ask You to heal me and make me strong in emotions, mind, and will. Please give me the courage to walk through life without the pain, insecurities, frustrations, and alienation I have been feeling. I trust You to set me free, make me whole, and keep me strong."

Today is a day for new beginnings toward a stronger tomorrow!

THE HOPE OF GREATER STRENGTH

A great deal has been written in recent years about inner healing, emotional wounds, and reversing low self-esteem. Bookstores are lined with self-help books. What so many people in our world do not realize is that the Bible has been the authoritative book on the healing and strengthening of the human soul (mind, emotions, will) for thousands of years. The Bible is not a self-help book but, rather, a God-will-help book. The Bible holds out the hope and promise of God's eternal help for the person who humbly turns to Him and says, "I cannot. You can. I put my trust in You for help."

When times of emotional pain or weakness come, we eventually reach the end of ourselves. There are those who teach that turning to God is a sign of emotional weakness in and of itself. The exact opposite is true. No person can fully heal his or her own spirit, soul, or body. Certain problems, difficulties, ailments, injuries, and conditions lie beyond a person's *capacity* to self-heal.

The good news for the Christian is that the end point of self is often the beginning point for God! The help that God offers us in His Word is both eternal and timely. It is highly effective and freely available to all.

How can we understand the help God offers? How can we avail ourselves of His healing and strengthening power? The Bible gives us the "ways and means" for receiving God's presence into our lives. The Bible is the reference to which we must return continually to determine what we must do when we feel weak, insecure, anxious, wounded, or broken.

I encourage you to keep your Bible close at hand as we move through this ten-part study. Make notes in the margins of your Bible as you look up various Scriptures and study them. It is far more important that you write God's insights into the Bible that you read daily than to write in this book, although places are provided here for you to make notes.

Keys to Study

At various times you will be asked to identify with the material of this study guide by answering one or more of these questions:

- What new insights have you gained?
- Have you ever had a similar experience?
- How do you feel about this?
- In what way are you feeling challenged to act?

Insights

A spiritual insight occurs when you see something as if for the first time. You may have read, studied, analyzed, or meditated on a particular passage many times—even to the point that you think there is nothing else you could possibly learn about it—and then God suddenly reveals new meaning to you. That is a spiritual insight.

Insights usually relate to something that you are experiencing or have experienced in your personal life. They give you an ability to apply God's Word in new ways. As such, they are part of God's unfolding wisdom to you (see James 1:5). Ask God to give you insights every time you open His Word to read it. I believe He'll answer that prayer.

I highly recommend that you note the insights you have into God's Word so that you might review them later in light of other Scriptures. In doing this, you will have your insights more readily available to share with others, and you will also find as you look back over your insights that your own faith is growing. Many people find that the more they are intentional and focused in looking and listening for insights, the more God gives insights.

Experiences

We each come to the Bible from a unique background—our personal histories and life experiences. As a result, we each have a unique perspective on what we read. Never dismiss the value of life experiences, even those experiences that may have been painful or difficult. Experience is part of the way God teaches us and molds us into conformity to Christ Jesus.

Our experiences to a great extent confirm to us the truth of the Bible. We can point to an incident in the past and say, "I know this Bible teaching is true because of what happened to me." The more we see the Bible as relating to our personal experiences, the more the Bible encourages, convicts, challenges, and transforms us. We grow in our understanding that, while God's Word is universal and applicable to all people in all ages, it is also highly individual and personal. There isn't anything that we encounter as human beings that isn't addressed by the Bible in one or more ways.

Certainly our life experiences don't *make* the Bible true. The Bible is truth, period. Our life experiences, however, do *confirm to us* that the Bible is true. The reality of God's Word "hits home" in the light of our experiences.

Sharing experiences in your journey of faith is essential for your spiritual growth. Even if you are doing this study on your own, I encourage you to talk to others about your faith experiences. Allow others to learn from you even as you learn from them.

This is especially important when sharing incidents concerning emotional pain or experiences that may be embarrassing to you. So many people today live with a sense of isolation; when they experience emotional pain they, too, often conclude, "I'm the only one who feels this way; I'm the only one who knows this pain." That is never the case. Invariably, there are others within a fairly small radius of friends and family members who have struggled or are struggling with that very problem. It is only when one person is willing to break the silence and talk about his inner pain, injury, or area of weakness, that help can flow freely and in a healing way among all members in a group setting. Don't be embarrassed by what you are feeling or have felt in the past. Sharing your emotional wounds will not only strengthen you, but may very well bring hope and help to another person.

As life experiences are shared—in fact, as insights, emotions, and convictions are shared—we must be committed as individuals and groups to keep confidential all that is shared in a group setting. Another person's story is just that—*his or her* story. It is not for you to retell without his or her express permission to do so. Neither should the experiences of one person be discussed by only a few of those in the group apart from the rest of the group, and definitely never apart from the person who initially shared his or her story. Don't assume that because a person shared a painful experience with a group, that this information is now public knowledge. It is not. Keep the confidences of the group. In that way, trust can grow and healing can be even more profound as communication within the group moves to deeper levels.

Emotional Response

Just as each person has unique experiences in life, so each of us has a unique emotional response to God's Word. No one emotional response is more valid than another. One person may be frightened or perplexed at what he reads. Another may feel great joy or relief in reading the same passage.

Face your own emotions honestly. And then be willing to share your emotions with others.

As in the case of life experiences, a strong emotional response to a passage of Scripture does not make the Bible true. Rather, our feelings and experiences provide evidence *to us* of the Bible's applicability and meaning to our individual lives.

Many people read the Bible with extreme objectivity, not allowing themselves to have an emotional response to the Scriptures. We are emotional people, however. God made us with emotions, and He desires for us to express them in appropriate ways. We must allow God's Word to touch our emotions and to bring about an emotional response in us if we are to be fully who He made us to be! At times, allow yourself to be moved to tears by what you read. At other times, allow yourself to feel great elation, conviction, hope, love, longing, surprise, or a host of other emotions. Any conversation that you have with another person has an emotional dimension. The Bible is God's "conversation" with you. Respond to it fully, including an emotional response.

In a group setting, you will find it much more beneficial to share emotions than to share opinions. Bible commentaries and Bible teaching have their place, but a group Bible study such as this one is a place to share experiences, personal insights, and feelings. Opinions tend to alienate and divide; emotional responses tend to bring about understanding and greater group empathy. None of us understand the Bible fully—it is a spiritual book that reflects the unfathomable riches of God's Spirit—but each of us has valid emotional responses and life experiences linked to God's Word. Keep your sharing limited to what you know with certainty at the deepest personal level.

Keep in mind as you progress through this study that those who have been deeply wounded emotionally tend to "shut down" their emotions. They seem to believe that if they can succeed in not feeling *anything,* they will be able to shut out the pain associated with their own memories. The greater reality related to the Scriptures is that when we open ourselves up to feeling emotions in the light of God's Word, the Holy Spirit can then work in and through our emotions to bring healing to that innermost part of us that has been injured or bruised. I have seen great healing occur through a free flow of tears, for example, after a person has held back tears for years and even decades.

At times, we discover that our emotional response to God's Word brings something to our conscious mind that has been buried in our subconscious. We have new insights into our own selves. These insights can be very helpful and meaningful if they are ones that compel a person to draw closer to God for healing, forgiveness, or renewal.

When dealing with a topic such as inner strength, and especially when sharing emotional responses within a group, a Bible study can easily get off track and become a "therapy group." Don't allow that to happen. Stay focused on what the Bible says. Let the Bible speak for itself, and allow it to speak to each person. Should emotions come to the surface, allow them to be expressed fully—thank God for their expression!—but then return quickly to your focus on the Scriptures.

Challenges

As we read the Bible, we need to come to the place where we feel challenged to *do something* in response to what we have read or studied. God is never content with our status quo. He is always working within us to conform us to the image of Christ Jesus and to help us "grow up" in our faith. Real growth comes not in merely understanding God's Word, as important as that is, but in *applying* God's Word to real-life situations and circumstances. The Bible challenges us to be doers of God's Word and not hearers only (see James 1:22).

We need to pinpoint, as best we can, the areas in which we believe God is challenging us, stretching us, or causing us to believe for more. When you can say to yourself at the conclusion of a period of Bible reading or Bible study, "This is what I believe God wants me to do," you are actually identifying your next step in spiritual growth. That is an exciting moment for each person. The real growth will occur, of course, when you actually follow through and *do* what the Lord is prompting you to do.

God's plan is a very simple one: He wants us to get into His Word so He can get His Word into us. Once we know God's Word, we are to share His Word with others, including those who don't know the Lord or who have never read the Bible. At other times we are called upon to share His Word with those who are fellow Christians and Bible students. The important thing is not with whom we share the Word as much as our willingness to share it openly and freely with as many people as possible, as the Lord leads us to share in His timing, and as He reveals to us His most effective methods. We are to be witnesses of the *full* truth He has revealed to us.

If you do not have somebody with whom you can discuss your spiritual insights, life experiences, emotional responses, and challenges, I encourage you to find somebody. Perhaps you can start a Bible study in your home. Perhaps you can talk to your pastor about organizing Bible study groups in your church. There is much to be learned on your own. There is much *more* to be learned as you become part of a small group that desires to grow in the Lord.

None of us are called to live or to struggle with our emotional pain and inner weaknesses on our own. We are called to be ministers of Christ *one to the other.* That is what it means to be the body of Christ, each person sharing fully his or her gifts, insights, and encouragement with other Christians in an active, ongoing manner.

Keep the Bible Central

At all times, keep the Bible itself central to your study. Gather around God's Word as if you are gathering around a dinner table—to draw spiritual nourishment from the Scriptures so that each person who partakes may grow in the Lord.

If you are doing a personal Bible study, be diligent in keeping your focus on God's Word. Self-analysis or personal recovery is not the goal of this study. Growing up into the fullness of the stature of Christ Jesus is the goal!

Prayer

Finally, I encourage you to begin and end your Bible study times in prayer. Ask God to give you spiritual eyes to see what He wants you to see and spiritual ears to hear what He wants you to hear. Ask Him to give you new insights, to remind you of pertinent life experiences that relate to what you read, to help you clarify your emotional responses to what you read, and to reveal to you what He desires for you to be, say, and do in response to His Word.

As you conclude your time of study, ask the Lord to seal what you have learned to your heart and mind so that you will never forget it. Ask Him to make you more like His Son, Jesus Christ, so that you will think, feel, speak, and act as Jesus would act if He were walking in your shoes and in your world today. Above all, ask the Lord to give you the courage to follow through and actually become, say, and do what He has challenged you to become, say, and do. Pray for boldness in sharing Christ with others.

And now, consider these questions at the outset of this study:

- *What new insights do you hope to gain through this study about emotional pain and inner weakness, and how God desires to impart His strength to every believer?*

_____

_____

- *In what areas have you struggled with emotional pain or injury in the past? Can you identify times when you have felt the need for greater inner strength?*

  _____

  _____

- *How do you feel about the prospect of being healed or strengthened in certain areas of your emotions?*

  _____

  _____

- *Are you open to God's healing of your emotional life or of past hurtful memories?*

  _____

  _____

STRENGTH IN TIMES OF LONELINESS

I clearly remember thinking as a child, *I have nobody.* There were many times when a feeling of utter loneliness would well up within me. It was a feeling that was all too familiar and that I carried with me at the core of my soul into adulthood.

Although the loneliness of my childhood may have been more severe than that experienced by many people, I know I am not alone in my experience. I have met hundreds—even thousands—of people through the years who have felt utterly alone, abandoned, isolated, ostracized, and thus, lonely.

Loneliness is one of the most excruciating feelings a person can ever have and one that nearly every person attempts to avoid at all costs. Even so, loneliness seems pervasive in our world today. Older people give frequent testimony to loneliness, especially after the death of a spouse. Divorced people feel lonely. Young people often think they are totally alone in their feelings, especially if they have indifferent, self-absorbed parents. Salespeople on the road are lonely. Mothers who stay at home all day with young children often speak of loneliness. College students and those who enter the military and are on their own for the first time are lonely. Those who have empty nests after years of raising children are lonely. Newly retired persons, accustomed to a wide circle of colleagues, are lonely. Loneliness abounds.

What does the Bible say to people who are lonely?

At the outset of the Bible, Genesis 1 through 3, we have a picture of the fellowship that God desires with human beings. He said, "Let Us make man in Our image, according to Our likeness" (Gen. 1:26). God displays an emotional capacity for companionship and a desire for it. Loneliness is not a desirable state, from God's point of view. Adam and Eve walked and talked with God frequently. His voice in the cool of the evening was not strange to them (see Gen. 3:8–9).

Time and again throughout the Old Testament, we find the Lord reaching out to His people, revealing Himself to them, desiring to be with them and to communicate with them. In 1 Samuel 12:22 we find this promise of God: "For the LORD will not forsake His people, for His great name's sake, because it has pleased the LORD to make you His people."

- *How do you feel about the idea that God desires to have fellowship with you and that one of His foremost reasons for creating you was precisely that He might have fellowship with you?*

_____

_____

Jesus Experienced Both Loneliness and Friendship

In the New Testament, we read how Jesus developed a very close relationship with a group of men we call apostles. He was so concerned that they continue in their relationship with one another even after His crucifixion that He spent much of His last night with them talking about their need to remain one with each other, and to be as one with the Father. We read in the Gospel of John,

- *[Jesus said], "Let not your heart be troubled; you believe in God, believe also in Me. In My Father's house are many mansions; if it were not so, I would have told you. I go to prepare a place for you. And if I go and prepare a place for you, I will come again and receive you to Myself; that where I am, there you may be also." (14:1–3)*
- *[Jesus said], "I will pray the Father, and He will give you another Helper, that He may abide with you forever—the Spirit of truth, whom the world cannot receive, because it neither sees Him nor knows Him; but you know Him, for He dwells with you and will be in you. I will not leave you orphans; I will come to you." (14:16–18)*
- *[Jesus said], "As the Father loved Me, I also have loved you; abide in My love." (15:9)*
- *[Jesus said], "This is My commandment, that you love one another as I have loved you. Greater love has no one than this, than to lay down one's life for his friends." (15:12–13)*

- *What new insights do you have into these four passages of Scripture?*
  John 14:1–3

_____

_____

John 14:16–18

_____

_____

John 15:9

_____

_____

John 15:12–13

_____

_____

The close communion that the Lord desires and is willing to experience with us is something we can count on, even if everyone else abandons us. Jesus knew this to be true in His own life. On the night He was arrested and tried—the trial that ended in His crucifixion—He said to His disciples, "Indeed the hour is coming, yes, has now come, that you will be scattered, each to his own, and will leave Me alone." Can you hear the pain in that statement? Jesus knew what it was to be lonely. But then Jesus went on to say, "And yet I am not alone, because the Father is with Me" (John 16:32). Jesus knew what it was to be comforted even in the face of abandonment.

- *How do you feel about the fact that Jesus was lonely on occasion for human companionship?*

_____

_____

The good news for every Christian is that Jesus is our Friend of friends. He is with us always and He never changes, abandons us, or withdraws from us. We can trust Him *always* to be present so that we never are truly alone.

What the Word Says	What the Word Says to Me
[Jesus said], "Lo, I am with you always, even to the end of the age." (Matt. 28:20)	_____ _____ _____
For I am persuaded that neither death nor life, nor angels nor principalities nor powers,	_____ _____ _____

nor things present nor things
to come, nor height nor depth,
nor any other created thing,
shall be able to separate us
from the love of God which is
in Christ Jesus our Lord.
(Rom. 8:38–39)

Feeling Alone vs. Truly Being Alone

Being alone is a blessing to some people who find that they are continually surrounded by people or people-related demands. For others, being alone brings about great feelings of loneliness. For still others, loneliness is so pervasive in their souls that they can feel lonely even in a room full of people.

One of the things you must continually guard your mind against is the idea that you are an isolated example or one-of-a-kind in your feelings of loneliness. The truth is that you are *never* alone; not only is the Holy Spirit present and available to you always, but there are many other Christian people who have experienced what you are experiencing and who would *like* the opportunity to be a friend to you. At times when we are lonely we simply need to reach out to others and invite their presence into our lives.

The prophet Elijah once felt very isolated and alone. He cried out to God, "The children of Israel have forsaken Your covenant, torn down Your altars, and killed Your prophets with the sword. I alone am left; and they seek to take my life" (1 Kings 19:14). Can you hear the desperation and loneliness in Elijah's words? Not only did he feel forsaken, but he felt that all of Israel had forsaken the things that were most important to Elijah.

The Lord responded to Elijah, "Go, return on your way to the Wilderness of Damascus . . . Yet I have reserved seven thousand in Israel, all whose knees have not bowed to Baal, and every mouth that has not kissed him" (1 Kings 19:15, 18). Not only was Elijah not truly alone as a follower of the Lord God and a keeper of God's covenant, but there were seven thousand people with whom he might associate!

The same is likely to be true for you. Not only are you not alone, but there are more people who feel as you feel and believe as you believe than you presently know! Seek them out.

- *What new insights do you have into 1 Kings 19:14–18?*

_____

_____

- *In what ways are you feeling challenged by the Holy Spirit to enrich or expand your circle of friends?*

_____

_____

Action to Take When You Feel Lonely

You simply cannot be alone once you have the Spirit of God dwelling in you. Even so, you can have a *feeling* of being alone even if you aren't alone. What, then, should you do when you have feelings of loneliness?

Lonely people seem to turn to many things that create more loneliness, rather than to those things that can alleviate their feelings. They turn to drugs and alcohol, both of which tend to alienate and turn away the very people with whom they might enjoy companionship. They sometimes turn to television, videos, or radio programs, all of which tend to isolate a person from human-to-human communication.

The foremost antidote that God has supplied for the person who feels lonely is this: good relationships with Christian people! The Lord said about Adam when He realized that Adam was alone, "It is *not* good that man should be alone," and then the Lord took the necessary step to resolve this situation, "I will make him a helper comparable to him" (Gen. 2:18). We often think this verse applies only to marriage but in a much broader sense, it applies to godly friendships. The Lord's desire is not only that you have a close, intimate relationship with Him but that you have satisfying and enriching personal relationships with other people.

• *Can you recall a period in your life when you felt lonely? What was the state of your friendships, or the availability of friends, during that time?*

_____

_____

How can we develop the friendships that will ease our feelings of loneliness? Proverbs 18:24 tells us, "A man who has friends must himself be friendly." Ask yourself today, "What kind of friend would I really like to have?" List below the traits that you desire in a friend:

_____

_____

_____

Now ask yourself an even more important question, "Am I willing to *be* this kind of friend?" To have a friend, you must be a friend.

Here are at least six things you can do to put yourself into the "market" for developing friendships:

1. Accept invitations to social events with godly people.

2. Get involved with your church and with various outreach ministries within your church. Be faithful in your attendance and in your participation in group functions. Serving the Lord in an active way with other believers is a wonderful way for friendships to develop.

3. Invite others to join you for lunch or after-church brunch.

4. Participate in retreats that are sponsored by your church or by Christian organizations, especially ones that involve other people who live in your city. Getting away for a weekend or going to a seminar with other Christians is a great way to meet people who are likely to have common interests with you.

5. Join Christian clubs or hobby groups—for example, a men's group that engages in outdoor activities or sports, a Christian businesswomen's group, an exercise class, or a theater group or choir attended by other Christians.

6. Attend a course offered by a local Christian college, Bible institute, or through your church. Studying with other Christians is a good way to make new friends who share an interest in similar topics. Sometimes "community learning programs" or "neighborhood schools" that offer nonacademic courses in such things as gourmet cooking, photography, or art appreciation are good places to meet potential friends.

Ask the Lord to reveal to you the people who may be your future friends. At the same time, ask Him to bring to your mind those friends whom you may have neglected recently; ask Him to show you ways in which you might rekindle old friendships. Is it right to ask God for friends? I encourage you to reflect upon 1 John 5:14–15:

Now this is the confidence that we have in Him, that if we ask anything according to His will, He hears us. And if we know that He hears us, whatever we ask, we know that we have the petitions that we have asked of Him.

Friendship is a good thing! It is God's will that you have friends. Therefore, when you ask the Lord to bring good

Christian friends into your life, you are asking something that is according to God's will. Look for God to bring people your way. Look for new opportunities to arise for you to be a friend, and in the process, to gain a friend.

- *What new insights do you have into 1 John 5:14–15 as these verses relate to friendship?*

———————————————————————

———————————————————————

In all things, remember Romans 8:28, which tells us that "all things work together for good to those who love God, to those who are the called according to His purpose." The good news of this verse applies to your friendships! God is the engineer of social relationships, and He has a way of bringing the right people into your life at the right times for the right purposes. Sometimes friendships last a lifetime. Sometimes they are intended only for a season of life. Trust God to bring you the friends you need right now and, in turn, to be a friend to those who need *your* friendship.

- *In the past, how have you met the people who became your close friends?*

———————————————————————

———————————————————————

- *How do you feel about the statement, "God is the engineer of social relationships"? Consider your friendships today and consider the fact that your friends are one of God's providential gifts to you.*

———————————————————————

———————————————————————

Do not give up on the Lord because you *feel* that He is distant from you. In reality, He is closer to you than your own breath.

What the Word Says	What the Word Says to Me
Let us consider one another in order to stir up love and good works, not forsaking the assembling of ourselves together. (Heb. 10:24–25)	------------------------------ ------------------------------ ------------------------------ ------------------------------ ------------------------------
Above all things have fervent love for one another . . . Be hospitable to one another. (1 Peter 4:8–9)	------------------------------ ------------------------------ ------------------------------ ------------------------------

Do not give up on a Christian friend because you *feel* that your friend has disappointed you, has withdrawn from you, or is in conflict with you. Ask your friend if you have done something to damage your friendship—for example, if you have erred in a way you do not realize you have erred, if you have required too much of your friendship, or if you have failed at being a good friend. If so, apologize to your friend and seek to make amends. Value your friendships enough to do your best to maintain them and develop them over time.

Keep in mind always that our own feelings sometimes deceive us. None of us have perfect perception, and especially so when we personally are involved. Ask the Holy Spirit to help you to build your life upon the truth of God's Word and the consistent reliability of God's presence and power. Feelings come and go. God's love, forgiveness, and presence with us are eternal and rock solid.

- *What new insights do you have into God's answer to loneliness?*

_____

_____

- *In what ways are you feeling challenged in your spirit today?*

_____

_____

STRENGTH IN TIMES OF FEAR

My insecurities and fears as a child were no doubt linked to the fact that I had relatively few things that I could count on as being consistent. We moved seventeen times in the first sixteen years of my life. We never really seemed to have enough, especially in my early years when my mother was struggling as a young widow to provide food and shelter for the two of us. Being solely responsible for an active, curious son, my mother was also very protective. She frequently said to me, "Don't fall down," "Watch out," "Be careful." The message to me was one of doom and gloom: "Don't take any risks, life is scary, and you're going to get hurt."

Furthermore, I was raised with the concept that God was a stern judge, just waiting to pounce on a little boy who might step out of line. From my earliest memories, I never dreamed of doing anything bad. I was too scared of the consequences! My entire outlook on life was one of deep emotional insecurity, anxiety, and fear. It took years of living with a full understanding of God's love, tenderness, and steadfast provision for me to overcome these negative emotions.

Again, I know that I am not alone in my experience with these emotions. Everywhere I look today, I find people living anxious lives. In fact, if we had only one word to describe our society it might be *anxious*. People aren't sure whom they can count on. The world seems to be changing rapidly on all fronts. Old moral and ethical standards in our culture seem to have fallen away fairly dramatically in recent years. Parents, stepparents, and foster parents seem to come and go in the lives of an increasing number of children; spouses seem more temporary than permanent in a number of people's lives. A life in which such fluctuations and changes are the norm is nearly always an *anxious* life.

- *Have you experienced times of anxiety or fear? What precipitated those times?*

  _____

  _____

- *Do you live with a pervasive feeling of anxiety? Have you considered the root causes for this feeling deep within your soul?*

  _____

  _____

The Root of Anxiety

Anxiety is fear of the future. We feel anxious when we come to the conclusion that the future holds no promise of change or when we aren't sure what's going to happen from one moment to the next.

Sometimes anxiety is rooted in a person's feelings that he is incapable of handling a new challenge.

At times, anxiety is rooted in a person's setting standards that are too high, even impossible.

Sometimes anxiety is rooted in a person's feeling torn between two opinions or between two people she loves.

At times, anxiety is rooted in unresolved hostility.

Jesus knew all about these causes of anxiety. Anxiety over life's basic needs was a problem when He walked the earth. Jesus lived in an area that was occupied by Rome, and nobody was ever sure what Rome might do next or what new taxes and laws might be issued against the Jews. Daily life was difficult: thousands upon thousands lived a hand-to-mouth, day-to-day existence. Sickness and disease were prevalent. Great tension existed between those who considered themselves to be "Law-keeping" Jews and those who were perceived to be Law-breakers.

This is what Jesus taught His disciples:

> Therefore I say to you, do not worry about your life, what you will eat; nor about the body, what you will put on. Life is more than food, and the body is more than clothing. Consider the ravens, for they neither sow nor reap, which have neither storehouse nor barn; and God feeds them. Of how much more value are you than the birds? And which of you by worrying can add one cubit to his stature? If you then are not able to do the least, why are you anxious for the rest? Consider the lilies, how they grow: they neither toil nor spin; and yet I say to you, even Solomon in all his glory was not arrayed like one of these. If then God so clothes the grass, which today is in the field and tomorrow is thrown into the oven, how much more will He clothe you, O you of little faith? And do not seek what you should eat or what you should drink, nor have an anxious mind. For all these things the nations of the world seek after, and your Father knows that you need these things. (Luke 12:22–30)

• *What new insights do you have into this passage of Scripture?*

_____

_____

As you look closely at what Jesus taught about anxiety, I hope you will note these three things:

1. *God knows what you need.* Much of our anxiety is rooted in a feeling that we must maintain control over every detail in our lives because there is nobody else whom we can trust to know our needs and to provide for us. Jesus made it very clear, "Your Father knows." He knows because He cares for us with an infinite love. We are of exceedingly great value to Him.

2. *God will supply what you need.* Not only does God know what you need, but He knows by what means, when, and precisely how much to supply you so that your need is met fully. He is a loving Father who desires the best for His children, which includes a full provision.

3. *Only God can alleviate fully your feelings of anxiety.* Nobody else can ever fully know or meet this need in your life. God alone sees the beginning from the ending of your life and, therefore, He alone knows what you will need at precisely every moment of your life in order for you to do the work and fulfill the plan that He has for you.

God will do the providing for us *as we trust Him.* His part is to meet our needs. Our part is to trust Him to meet our needs.

What the Word Says	What the Word Says to Me
[Jesus said], "Seek the kingdom of God, and all these things shall be added to you." (Luke 12:31)	----------------------------- ----------------------------- ----------------------------- -----------------------------
God shall supply all your need according to His riches in glory by Christ Jesus. (Phil. 4:19)	----------------------------- ----------------------------- ----------------------------- -----------------------------

• *How do you feel when you know that provision or help is on the way? How might this feeling relate to your faith?*

_____

_____

The Need for a Personal Relationship with Christ

The first and foremost step to overcoming anxiety is to make certain that you have a personal relationship with Jesus Christ. To do that, you need to come sincerely and honestly to God and say, "I want to have a relationship with You. I accept what You have done for me—that You have sent Jesus Christ to this earth to die in my place and to be the sacrifice for my sins. I accept that You desire to have a relationship with me. I receive today the free gift of Your grace that You have made available to me. I choose to follow the Lord."

Until Jesus is a part of your life, you will always fear the unknown.

Once you are born anew in your spirit and have a relationship with Jesus Christ, you must actively acknowledge the fact that the Holy Spirit is resident in you. And you must ask the Holy Spirit to lead, guide, and empower you daily to live the life the Lord is asking you to live. I encourage you to pray daily, "Father, I receive the gift of Your Holy Spirit to help me today to say and do what is pleasing to You, and to do so with a right spirit, in right timing, and according to right methods. Lead and guide my every step today."

Every person has moments of anxiety and fear in his or her life. But a pervasive feeling of anxiousness and fearfulness is *not* God's desire for any person. Put your faith in what God has done for you by sending Jesus to this earth on your behalf. Place your trust in the Holy Spirit to lead you along life's path with confidence and hope.

What the Word Says	What the Word Says to Me
I can do all things through Christ who strengthens me. (Phil. 4:13)	------------------------------ ------------------------------ ------------------------------
I will instruct you and teach you in the way you should go; I will guide you with My eye. (Ps. 32:8)	------------------------------ ------------------------------ ------------------------------ ------------------------------
Trust in the LORD with all your heart, And lean not on your own understanding; In all your ways acknowledge Him, And He shall direct your paths. (Prov. 3:5–6)	------------------------------ ------------------------------ ------------------------------ ------------------------------ ------------------------------ ------------------------------ ------------------------------

- *In what way are you feeling challenged today?*

_____

_____

What Happens If We Don't Trust God?

If we choose not to trust God fully with our lives, then we are left with the options of trusting either ourselves or other people with our lives. A person doesn't need to live very long before he concludes that no one person can fully care for himself, and no other person or institution can be relied upon fully to provide all that any one person needs. Only God, who has all resources available for His use, can put together a "total provision package" for each person on earth.

If we choose not to trust God fully with our lives, the results often include:

- Increased irritability and frustration with life
- A continual vacillation of opinion and little deci-
  sion making
- Repeated errors of judgment
- Feelings of persecution, even if no persecutor can
  be named
- Procrastination
- Increased use of chemicals (such as alcohol, drugs,
  and overuse of prescription medications) to escape
  pain, sleeplessness, or nervous tension
- Low productivity
- A general feeling of restlessness or uneasiness

Jesus referred to such consequences as these in a parable,
saying,

> Behold, a sower went out to sow. And as he sowed, some
> seed . . . fell among thorns, and the thorns sprang up
> and choked them . . . Now he who received seed among
> the thorns is he who hears the word, and the cares of
> this world and the deceitfulness of riches choke the
> word, and he becomes unfruitful. (Matt. 13:3–4, 7, 22)

Those things that cause anxiety in us are what Jesus refers
to as "the cares of this world." They choke the Word of God.
What does this mean? It means that a person who becomes
self-absorbed with situations, circumstances, and self-pursuits
is not fully capable of taking into his thoughts and emotions
the Word of God. He allows the mundane responsibilities of
life to overwhelm him to the point that he gives no thought to
God's promises, much less relies upon them as pertaining to
his life.

How can we reverse this trend? The Scriptures say that we
must take every thought that is contrary to the Word of God
"captive." We must recognize our self-absorbed thoughts, cap-
ture them, and literally force them into submission, saying to

ourselves, "I will not think about this. Rather, I will think about what God says in His Word. I will focus completely and totally on the truth of God, not the facts and opinions that others are feeding to me about my situation or circumstances."

What other people tell us always has an element of error in it (because it is rooted in humanity or tainted by human frailty), and it is temporary (because no person can see the entire future or past of our lives). What we read in God's Word is true and eternal.

Paul admonished the Corinthians that they were to use their weapons of spiritual warfare for "casting down arguments and every high thing that exalts itself against the knowledge of God, bringing every thought into captivity to the obedience of Christ" (2 Cor. 10:5).

How do we do this in a practical way?

When times of anxiety and fear seem to overwhelm you, you must make a conscious, deliberate effort to take control over your own thoughts and to bring them into conformity with God's Word. I encourage you to take these five steps:

1. *Read the Gospels.* Calm your own spirit by reading aloud the words of Jesus and the stories about Jesus in the Gospel books: Matthew, Mark, Luke, and John. Focus especially on what Jesus taught and said. (You may find it beneficial to use a Bible with the words of Jesus highlighted in red.) Don't allow yourself to become distracted or to give up in your reading of God's Word until you feel panic subside and a calmness take root in your heart.

2. *Read the promises of God to you.* Begin to look up and read aloud the promises of God's Word that pertain to your situation. If you don't know those promises, use a concordance to find them. (Look up a word that relates to your problem, or look up those passages under the heading "fear not.")

3. *Memorize God's promises.* Memorize several of God's promises that seem especially appropriate for your particular situation. As you read the Bible daily and you discover other promises or passages that seem appropriate to your particular

situation, memorize them also. Any time fear attempts to rise up in you again, recite these promises from God's Word—repeatedly, if need be—until the fear subsides.

4. *Ask the Holy Spirit to take control.* Ask the Holy Spirit to bring the promises in God's Word to the fullness of reality in your life. Ask Him to take control of your life and to take control over the situations that are causing you to fear or to feel anxious.

5. *Praise God.* Begin to praise God for His greatness, goodness, and tender loving care of you in the past. Recall instances in which God has shown Himself to be faithful. Recall instances in which your needs were met, your heart was blessed, and you knew with a surety that God was in control of your life. Praise God for His provision and presence in the past.

And then, continue to praise God for who He *is*—that He is *always faithful,* which means that what He has done in the past, He will do in the present and the future. Praise God for His *goodness*—that He can and does work all things together for your eternal good. Praise God for His *love* that is infinitely deeper and more wonderful than you can fathom.

As a whole and when executed with faith that God *will* take care of you, this discipline puts a stop to a buildup of anxiety in your life. It reverses the spiraling trend that can so quickly plunge a person into panic or confusion! It pulls your mind and heart back into a proper focus on Jesus Christ and what He did for you on the cross, on the Holy Spirit and what He does for you daily, and on God's power to strengthen you and take care of you now and forever. It gives you a basis in which to root your hope and faith. And, it invites the Holy Spirit to deal in a more active and potent way in and through you right in the midst of your anxiety.

I encourage you to engage in this fivefold process as often as anxiety or fear takes hold of you. You may need to devote a period of time each day to doing this discipline of reading, reciting, praying, and praising—even several periods of time each day—in order to defeat a pervasive feeling of anxiety or fear. Most of us did not become anxious in a moment, and most of us will not cease to feel anxious instantaneously.

What the Word Says	What the Word Says to Me
Submit to God. Resist the devil and he will flee from you. Draw near to God and He will draw near to you. (James 4:7–8)	----------------------------
Humble yourselves under the mighty hand of God, that He may exalt you in due time, casting all your care upon Him, for He cares for you. (1 Peter 5:6–7)	----------------------------

Finally, do not become discouraged if your ability to trust God seems to wax and wane. That is only human. Our ability to trust in God is never absolute, constant, perfect, or full. Rather, we are to *grow* in our ability to trust God. The decision we are challenged to make is to seek to trust God more. In times of weakness, we need to begin to trust Him. When our trust level is low, we need to trust Him more. Even in times of great trust, we must seek to trust Him *even more*. The wonderful hope that we have, of course, is that the more we trust God, the more we find God to be faithful. Thus, the more we are willing to trust, the more God shows us that we can trust Him.

God's nature has not changed. He is always trustworthy. What happens, rather, is that we grow in our ability to trust Him. We have greater inner strength to trust. The more we cast our cares upon Him, the more He shows us how much He truly desires to care for us, give to us, and deliver us from all harm.

- *What new insights do you have into God's provision of strength for you in the face of anxiety and fear?*

  _____

  _____

- *In what ways are you feeling challenged in your spirit today?*

  _____

  _____

STRENGTH IN TIMES OF ABUSE

When I was nine years old, my mother married my stepfather, a man who was full of hostility, anger, and bitterness. Never once did I hear this man say that he cared for me or loved me. I don't recall his ever giving me anything. What I do recall with vivid memories are the times when he blew up in anger. He was so abusive that many nights as a teenager I went to bed with a rifle loaded beside me and the door locked.

Countless adults today can relate to my experiences. It seems that in the last two decades, the willingness of our society to admit, confront, and talk about abuse has greatly increased.

The definition of abuse, however, tends to vary from one person to the next. The extent of *perceived* abuse can also vary from one period in life to the next. Verbal and emotional abuse are more difficult to define than physical or sexual abuse. What is important for our discussion here is that we recognize a fundamental difference between discipline and abuse.

Discipline is given in direct response to a person's actions. It is administered for the ultimate benefit of the person being disciplined; the goal of discipline is altered behavior and a change in the way a person responds to life. Discipline is an act of love; it is rooted in a desire for a person to be the best that a person can be.

Abuse, in sharp contrast, is frequently unrelated to a victim's behavior. A victim's totally innocent actions may trigger a violent response in an abuser. Abuse seeks to do a victim harm, to inflict pain. It is not corrective. And most important, abuse is manipulative and based on power. At the core of abusive behavior is a desire to control someone else.

We can be certain about two things:

1. It is never God's desire that His children be ritualistically or regularly injured emotionally or physically. Intense verbal criticism, beatings, and instances of severe deprivation of basic needs are *not* God's plan for any person.

2. It is never God's desire that His children be sexually abused. Incest, adultery, and fornication are all explicitly forbidden in the Scriptures.

God is never to blame in abusive situations. The blame rests solely with the abuser, and if any underlying spiritual motivation is at work, it comes from the devil, not God. Jesus said clearly, "The thief [the devil] does not come except to steal, and to kill, and to destroy. I have come that they may have life, and that they may have it more abundantly" (John 10:10). God never causes or motivates a person toward abusive behavior.

Responses to Abusive Behavior

How, then, should a Christian respond to abusive behavior from another person?

The Bible gives us at least six specific things we can do. All of them put us into a position for the Lord to heal us from any damage that has been done to us emotionally and to free us so that we are able to move forward in our lives without carrying the heavy baggage that results from abuse.

1. Seek God's Guidance

Ask the Lord, "What would You have me to do?" No one answer fits all situations. In some cases, God may tell you to move away physically from your abuser. In some cases, the Lord may direct you to receive wise counseling from a Bible-honoring, objective counselor. In still other cases, God may ask you to stay in a relationship with an abusive person and to pray for that person, believing for a transformation in the life of the abuser and your relationship. You will need to ask the Lord for His plan for *you*.

Go to the Lord in prayer, believing that He will direct your path and give you the courage to follow the plan He reveals to you.

What the Word Says	What the Word Says to Me
[Jesus said], "Ask, and it will be given to you; seek, and you will find; knock, and it will be opened to you. For everyone who asks receives, and he who seeks finds, and to him who knocks it will be opened." (Matt. 7:7–8)	_____ _____ _____ _____ _____ _____ _____ _____
If any of you lacks wisdom, let him ask of God, who gives to all liberally and without reproach, and it will be given to him. But let him ask in faith, with no doubting. (James 1:5–6)	_____ _____ _____ _____ _____ _____ _____

- *Recall an instance of abuse in your life or in the life of a person you know. How did the Lord lead this person to respond?*

_____

_____

- *What happened as a result of his or her obedience to the Lord?*

_____

_____

2. Pray for Your Abuser

The person who abuses you is a persecutor not only of you, but of Christ who dwells within you. As you pray for an abuser, ask the Lord to give you insights into the cause of the abusive behavior; these causes can help you as you intercede in prayer for the person. I learned later in my life that my stepfather had a deep anger against his own father because he had been denied an opportunity to pursue the career he wanted as a young man. Knowing this did not change my stepfather, nor did it lessen my abhorrence for the abuse I experienced. It did, however, give me a greater compassion to pray for my stepfather.

Pray specifically that your abuser will come into a relationship with the Lord Jesus and that the Lord will deal with the heart of this person. Also pray for boldness to confront your abuser with the message, "That's enough." Abusers expect their victims to run away and hide, cry, shrink back, or fall silent. One of the most beneficial things you can do for yourself as a victim is to stand up to your abuser and say, "I am a child of God. I will no longer take your abuse. I'm trusting God to defend me. I'm turning you over to Him, and I'm trusting that He will deal with you."

What the Word Says	What the Word Says to Me
[Jesus said], "You have heard that it was said, 'You shall love your neighbor and hate your enemy.' But I say to you, love your enemies, bless those who	_____ _____ _____ _____ _____

curse you, do do good to those
who hate you, and pray for
those who spitefully use you
and persecute you, that you
may be sons of your Father in
heaven." (Matt. 5:43–45)

If your enemy is hungry, give
him bread to eat; And if he is
thirsty, give him water to
drink; For so you will heap
coals of fire on his head, and
the Lord will reward you.
(Prov. 25:21–22)

- *In your experience, what happens inside your own heart when you pray for a person who has wronged you?*

_____

_____

3. Forgive Your Abuser

Choose to forgive not only the person who has abused you, but also any person who you believe contributed to or "stood by" as you were abused. Forgiveness does not mean that the abuse didn't happen, nor does it mean that the abuse was not an important issue in your life. What it means is that you are "letting go" of any anger, hurt, bitterness, or residual pain associated with the abuse you have experienced and you are trusting God to deal with your abuser. Forgiveness is an act of releasing the person—not to "go free" without any consequences for his or her behavior, but rather, releasing the person into the hands of the Lord and *His* consequences.

Part of forgiveness means not taking revenge into your own hands. Refuse to retaliate against your abuser. Leave all acts of vengeance to God.

What the Word Says	What the Word Says to Me
[Jesus said], "Forgive, and you will be forgiven." (Luke 6:37)	------------------------------ ------------------------------
[Jesus said], "If you forgive men their trespasses, your heavenly Father will also forgive you. But if you do not forgive men their trespasses, neither will your Father forgive your trespasses." (Matt. 6:14–15)	------------------------------ ------------------------------ ------------------------------ ------------------------------ ------------------------------ ------------------------------ ------------------------------

• *How do you feel about God's command to forgive those who abuse you, and to pray for those who persecute you?*

_____

_____

4. Open Yourself to God's Healing

Many people who have been abused continue to suffer from nightmares or a sudden onslaught of overwhelming memories for years, or even decades, after the abuse occurred. If you are experiencing these abused emotions, it is vitally important that you develop a habit of filling your mind with God's Word, especially just before you go to bed at night. Listen to messages—either spoken or in song—that fill your mind with God's Word and statements of God's love, goodness, grace, and kindness toward you. You may want to listen to Bible tapes or read aloud from God's Word. If memories of abuse haunt you, address them in the name of Jesus, saying, "Lord, I'm trusting You to turn my thoughts toward what is good, right, and beneficial for me." Speak to your dreams or memories: "You are not of God, and you no longer have a place in my mind. I give you to Christ Jesus, and I choose to think of what He has done for me rather than what has been done to me by others."

Ask the Lord to replace your bad memories of abuse with positive images of the ways in which the Lord has extended His love to you through others.

What the Word Says	What the Word Says to Me
Whatever things are true, whatever things are noble, whatever things are just, whatever things are pure, whatever things are lovely, whatever things are of good report, if there is any virtue and if there is anything praiseworthy—meditate on these things. (Phil. 4:8)	_____ _____ _____ _____ _____ _____ _____ _____ _____
Do not be overcome by evil, but overcome evil with good. (Rom. 12:21)	_____ _____ _____

• *In your experience, what "good things" can you cite to counteract negative images and feelings associated with abusive behavior you may have experienced?*

_____

_____

5. Choose to Pursue the Truth About Yourself

Those who are abused nearly always come to believe lies about themselves at some point. They believe that they deserve the abuse, that they are unworthy of love, that they are worthless, or that they are inept or incapable of succeeding in life. These are all lies, and they need to be labeled as such!

The truth needs to be proclaimed aloud *by the victim of abuse:* "The truth is that I can do all things through Christ Jesus. I am a joint heir in Christ Jesus of all God's benefits. I am in line to receive God's rewards. Christ in me has the power, strength, and ability, and together we will succeed in this."

Each of us has room for growth and improvement, but the abuser rarely focuses on specific areas of fault or error. Rather, an abuser issues generalized "labels" to his victims, using such phrases as, "You always," "You never," or "You will never." Labels such as these are a sure indicator that a lie is being told because the truth of God is that we *can* always become more than we are today, we *can* be forgiven, and that God holds out hope for us that tomorrow can be brighter than today. Every time a negative self-criticism comes to mind or is heard from another, the abused person needs to respond, "That's a lie! I will not believe that. It isn't true according to God's Word."

What the Word Says	What the Word Says to Me
These . . . things the LORD hates, . . . A false witness who speaks lies, And one who sows discord among brethren. (Prov. 6:16, 19)	_____ _____ _____ _____ _____
[Jesus said], "The devil . . . was a murderer from the beginning, and does not stand in the truth, because there is no truth in him. When he speaks a lie, he speaks from his own resources, for he is a liar and the father of it." (John 8:44)	_____ _____ _____ _____ _____ _____ _____ _____ _____

• *What do you know to be true about yourself?*

_____

_____

6. Move Forward in Your Life Positively

Believe God will bring something good out of your past experience. Never let an abuser dictate the course of your life or keep you from doing what you know the Lord is leading you to do. Part of moving forward in your life is believing that the cycle of abuse in your family has been broken—and is being broken—by your change of behavior. We each are called to say, "That may be the way I was or the situation I was in, but I am redeemed by Christ Jesus. I am in the process of being transformed into His image. I am in the process of being healed."

Trust God to bring something good out of an abusive situation or a past experience of abuse. The Lord truly can create something wonderful in you and through you, no matter how you may have been hurt by others in the past. He can make you strong where you are weak, whole in areas where you feel shattered, and healthy in areas where you have been injured.

What the Word Says	What the Word Says to Me
We know that all things work together for good to those who love God, to those who are the called according to His purpose. (Rom. 8:28)	------------------------------- ------------------------------- ------------------------------- ------------------------------- -------------------------------
I can do all things through Christ who strengthens me. (Phil. 4:13)	------------------------------- ------------------------------- -------------------------------
Let the weak say, "I am strong." (Joel 3:10)	------------------------------- -------------------------------

- *How do you feel about the Lord's ability to use you and to bless you, even though you were once the victim of abusive behavior?*

_____

_____

Speaking God's Love to Yourself

If you are a victim of abuse, let me be the first to assure you: you are loved by God. You are loved by your fellow Christians. You are worthy to be loved . . . not because of what you have done, not because of what has been done to you, but because of who you are—a child of God, fully adopted into His family, and fully deserving of the love of your fellow brothers and sisters in Christ Jesus.

If nobody else is around you to speak the Lord's love into your life, I encourage you to speak God's love to yourself today. Say aloud, "I am God's child. He loves me—yes, me!" Let the truth of those words sink deep into your soul. Let them heal the hurt you have known and the shame you may have felt. Let God's love for you wipe away your tears and restore you to wholeness.

- *What new insights do you have into the strength that the Lord offers to those who have experienced abuse?*

_____

_____

- *In what ways are you feeling challenged in your spirit today?*

_____

_____

STRENGTH IN TIMES OF CRITICISM

Each of us experiences criticism from time to time. In some cases it is a part of discipline to teach us how to improve in a particular skill, attitude, or behavior. Pervasive criticism, however, can have a wounding and weakening effect.

Through much of my childhood, I received numerous messages that reinforced the idea to me that I wasn't good for anything, wasn't worth anything, and would never amount to anything. I tried very hard to please, but several factors seemed to work against me in those days. One of the factors was that I had started school a year before my peers so I was always the youngest person in my class; therefore, I also tended to be the smallest and skinniest. Another factor was that my mother made me wear short pants until I went to junior high school, and then I wore knickers and long socks. Nobody else wore knickers! Yet another factor was that I grew up in a poor environment. Several of our apartments were in the basements of buildings. From my perspective as a child, everybody was "higher" than we were.

To counterbalance these negative messages, I also had some positive self-esteem-building influences—in particular a school-teacher named Mrs. Ferrell and a Sunday school teacher named Craig Stowe. These two people gave me important signs of approval when I needed them desperately. They were like beacons in a wilderness of disapproval.

Many people carry emotional baggage associated with intense or pervasive criticism. They express it by saying, "Nobody cared," "I never heard a word of praise when I was growing up," or "Nobody ever said to me, 'Good job.'" They express the criticism they heard as children in a wide variety of self-demeaning actions or in self-deprecating statements.

Perhaps the foremost thing we need to recognize about those who have been weakened by years of critical comment is that criticism *damages* a person on the inside. It wounds a person in his emotions.

- *Have you or someone you love been the recipient of ongoing, long-lasting, or intense criticism? What happens to the emotions and inner courage of a person who is severely criticized over a prolonged period of time?*

_____

_____

Get the Right Opinion

Criticism is nearly always registered at what a person *isn't doing right* or what a person *doesn't have enough of that is good.* A perceived lack of goodness brings about a perceived act or state of badness. It is no wonder that those who are criticized over a long period come to the conclusion, "I'm worthless. I'm no good. I can't make it. I'll never do any better." They have been fed a message of what they *aren't* so often and to such a great degree that they have lost all sight of what they *are.*

The first step toward overcoming the emotional wounds of criticism is to get the right perspective on one's self-worth. If we continue to hold a feeling of inadequacy and low self-value, we are denying what God Himself says about us.

On the other hand, when we set our eyes on who God says we are and what God thinks about us, self-esteem automatically begins to rise.

God bases our worth not on *what* we have, but on *whom* we have—Jesus Christ as our personal Savior and the Holy Spirit as our ever-present Comforter and Counselor. If you have accepted Jesus Christ as your Savior and have received the Holy Spirit into your life, you have *all that it takes* to have everlasting value in God's eyes!

God bases our worth not on our performance or achievements, but on whether we have received His free gift of grace and forgiveness in our lives.

God bases our worth not on where we live or how we look, but on whether we know, follow, and trust Jesus Christ as our Lord.

As long as a person bases his self-value on personal achievements, associations, or acquisitions, value will remain low. When a person bases his self-value on his relationship with God, value soars!

When we look at what we have done and can do by ourselves, we inevitably come to the conclusion that we are lacking in ability. When we look, however, at all that God desires for us to do, equips us to do, and promises to enable us to do, we lack no ability!

When it comes to who you are and what you are destined to do in life, there's only one opinion that truly matters—the Lord's opinion!

What Is the Lord's Opinion of You?

The Lord says that you are His workmanship. This means that you are a person of notable excellence solely because *He made you.* You are a prized example of His creation. In every case cited in Genesis, God looked at all that He made and declared, "It is good." That's the way the Lord looks upon you as His creation. He doesn't make inferior or worthless human beings. The Lord is a master Craftsman who produces only valuable people.

The Lord says that He removed your sin nature the moment you believed in Christ Jesus as your Savior. The only thing about your creation that can keep you from fully experiencing the presence of God is the sin nature with which you were born. Once you have received Christ Jesus as your Savior, that sin nature has been changed. You are "born again" with a new spiritual nature that puts you into a completely reconciled relationship with God. The one negative aspect of your being has been removed forever! Not only are you valuable to the Lord as His creation, but you are also forgiven and gain full status as one whom the Lord can use and bless fully for His purposes.

The Lord says that He has created and saved you for a future of good works. The Lord has already designed what those good works are to be. God had a purpose in mind for you even before you were born. He has a role for you to fill, a niche for you to occupy, and a place for you to live as His person on this earth. Furthermore, with the Holy Spirit resident in you, the Lord declares that you are equipped, empowered, and enabled to succeed in all that He calls you to do.

- *Have you come to a place in your life where you know without any doubt that you are God's creation, God's beloved son or daughter (through the forgiveness made possible by Jesus Christ), and that you have a destiny of good works planned by God?*

_____

_____

What the Word Says

If anyone is in Christ, he is a new creation; old things have

What the Word Says to Me

----

passed away; behold, all things
have become new. (2 Cor.
5:17)

I have been crucified with
Christ; it is no longer I who
live, but Christ lives in me; and
the life which I now live in the
flesh I live by faith in the Son
of God, who loved me and
gave Himself for me. (Gal.
2:20)

Let no one deceive you with
empty words, for because of
these things the wrath of God
comes upon the sons of dis-
obedience. Therefore do not be
partakers with them. For you
were once darkness, but now
you are light in the Lord. Walk
as children of light (for the
fruit of the Spirit is in all goodness, righteousness, and truth),
finding out what is acceptable
to the Lord. (Eph. 5:6–10)

Refuse to Perpetuate a Cycle of Criticism

As is the case in a number of areas of emotional wounding,
the person who is hurt has a built-in human tendency to hurt
others in the same area. Those who are criticized harshly and
for a long period of time tend to be more critical of others or
to continue the pattern of criticism by downgrading themselves.

Ask the Lord to help you put a stop to both patterns.

Refuse to ridicule others. Instead, choose to praise and encourage others, building up their strengths. Focus on their assets and positive attributes, rather than their deficits and flaws. The person who praises the good work of the Lord in others is an "edifier"—one who builds up others and encourages them in their faith walk. We are called repeatedly in the Scriptures to be edifiers.

Refuse to downgrade yourself in the presence of others or to engage in behaviors that send a message that you do not care about your appearance, your reputation, or your responsibilities.

What the Word Says	What the Word Says to Me
[Jesus said], "Judge not, and you shall not be judged. Condemn not, and you shall not be condemned." (Luke 6:37)	_____
Let all bitterness, wrath, anger, clamor, and evil speaking be put away from you, with all malice. And be kind to one another, tenderhearted, forgiving one another, even as God in Christ forgave you. (Eph. 4:31–32)	_____

- *In what ways are you feeling challenged in your spirit to break a cycle of criticism?*

_____

_____

Get the Right Perspective on Perfection

One of the consequences of those who experience years of criticism, and who in turn develop low self-esteem or an inferiority complex, is that they strive for perfection in an effort to prove themselves worthy or valuable to others. The perfectionist is usually a person who is less likely to appraise abilities and attributes realistically. Feeling that she is worth nothing and incapable of anything but failure, the perfectionist then seeks to succeed at all costs.

The truth is that nobody can live up to God's perfection. Nobody can "get it right" all the time. Nobody can live a totally sin-free life. Nobody can escape all temptation. Romans 3:23 clearly states, "All have sinned and fall short of the glory of God."

You may ask, "But what about those verses in the Bible that call us to be perfect?" When the Bible speaks of perfection, it is referring to what we call "wholeness" today. To be perfect, a person would have to be whole, and the converse is equally true from the Bible's perspective: to be made whole is to be made perfect. God calls us to pursue wholeness at all times. But, the Lord also tells us plainly in His Word that He is the One who makes us whole; we cannot make ourselves whole. The way to "perfection," therefore, is to trust God to do His perfecting work in us. We are not to struggle to become perfect, strive for perfection, or knock ourselves out trying to get everything right all the time. He'll do the work in us and bring about His perfection in His timing, using His methods, and all for His purposes.

In 1 John 2:1 we read, "My little children, these things I write to you, that you may not sin." But then the verse continues, "And if anyone sins, we have an Advocate with the Father, Jesus Christ the righteous." It's as if God is saying to us, "Little children, I don't want you to sin. I've given you My Word so that you can grow up and avoid sinning. But if and when you sin, I've made provision for that too."

We can't be perfect and we won't ever be perfect, but we can enjoy the perfection of Christ Jesus at work in us. We can accept His loving-kindness. We can acknowledge the presence and power of the Holy Spirit to help us in all things. We can place our trust in a perfect God who promises to be both the Author and the Finisher of our lives.

Recognize that you aren't who you once were, and that the Lord is continuing to mold and make you. Trust Him to be your potter (see Jer. 18:1–6).

What the Word Says	What the Word Says to Me
[The Lord spoke to Paul], "My grace is sufficient for you, for My strength is made perfect in weakness." (2 Cor. 12:9)	_____
The word which came to Jeremiah from the LORD, saying: "Arise and go down to the potter's house, and there I will cause you to hear My words." Then I went down to the potter's house, and there he was, making something at the wheel. And the vessel that he made of clay was marred in the hand of the potter; so he made it again into another vessel, as it seemed good to the potter to make. Then the word of the LORD came to me, saying: "O house of Israel, can I not do with you as this potter?" says the LORD. "Look, as the clay is in the potter's hand, so are you in My hand, O house of Israel!" (Jer. 18:1–6)	_____

- *In what ways can you reflect on your life and see how God has "developed" who you are today?*

_____

_____

- *In what ways are you feeling challenged about a tendency you may have toward perfectionism?*

_____

_____

Have the Right Desire to Please

Those who have suffered from criticism, and have developed a feeling of inferiority as a result, often have a great desire to "please" others—they go above and beyond the call of duty in trying to serve, thereby gaining the approval of those they perceive to be in authority over them.

As Christians, we are always called to do our best, within the framework of the talents, gifts, and abilities God has given us. We are not, however, called to

- compare ourselves to others, hoping that "in comparison," we will look better, or
- seek the approval of men and women if that approval is contrary to God's commandments.

God doesn't grade on the curve. He always judges our behavior against the absolute standard of His commandments. Furthermore, God is not merciful to us on the basis of whether other people like us, but solely on the basis of our acceptance of Jesus Christ and the forgiveness made possible to us through His shed blood. We gain nothing by comparing ourselves to others or in seeking to win popularity among our peers.

A desire to please God is manifested in three main ways:

1. A desire to allow the Holy Spirit to transform us.

2. A willingness to trust God to lead us where He chooses, and to use us in ways that He designs.

3. A commitment to doing what the Lord calls us to do, even if it is contrary to the norms of the world.

To truly please God, we must be willing to change and to grow ever more into the likeness of Jesus Christ. We must be willing to go wherever the Lord leads us and to do whatever He puts in our path to do.

The Lord doesn't ask us to succeed in the eyes of others, but He does ask us to live a life that is acceptable to Him.

Jesus never said, "Do your best." He said, "Follow Me." If we truly desire to please the Lord, we *will* follow Him and become His disciples.

What the Word Says

Do not be conformed to this world, but be transformed by the renewing of your mind, that you may prove what is that good and acceptable and perfect will of God. (Rom. 12:2)

The LORD is my shepherd;
I shall not want.
He makes me to lie down in green pastures;
He leads me beside the still waters.
He restores my soul;
He leads me in the paths of righteousness
For His name's sake.

What the Word Says to Me

Yea, though I walk through the
valley of the shadow of death,
I will fear no evil;
For You are with me;
Your rod and Your staff, they
comfort me.
You prepare a table before me
in the presence of my enemies;
You anoint my head with oil;
My cup runs over.
Surely goodness and mercy
shall follow me All the days of
my life;
And I will dwell in the house
of the LORD Forever. (Ps. 23)

I beseech you therefore,
brethren, by the mercies of
God, that you present your
bodies a living sacrifice, holy,
acceptable to God, which is
your reasonable service. (Rom.
12:1)

- *What new insights do you have into the way the Lord desires to strengthen those who have been weakened by criticism?*

  _____

  _____

- *In what ways are you feeling challenged in your spirit today?*

  _____

  _____

STRENGTH IN TIMES OF GUILT

Most people develop their God concept upon the behavior of their parents. My father died when I was nine months old, and when he died, a little bit of my concept about God was established that said, in effect, "God has left you too." My mother worked full-time, and I spent many hours alone after school. I came to believe, "God is away somewhere with somebody else."

God was remote to me, and He was a hard, harsh God from my perspective as a lonely, anxious, insecure child. He was authority—and in that regard, He was very much like my stepfather: mean, abusive, out to put me down and drive me out.

I had seen God's hand at work in my church and in my grandfather's life to the point that I had the faith to believe in God. I knew the Bible stories well enough to know about Jesus and what He had done in giving His life on the cross. Still, God was such a mystery that I never truly felt He was accessible to me. I had a strong feeling that I needed to be more holy so that God might come closer.

No matter how much I read the Bible, I felt I could have read it more. No matter how much I prayed, I felt I could have prayed more. I felt certain that God was keeping score on every aspect of my behavior. And the end result was the heavy emotional baggage of pervasive guilt.

Through the years, many people have told me that they have had a similar experience in their lives. They have spent years trying

- to get good enough for God to approve of them,
- to perform for God so that He might reward them, and
- to do enough good works so that they can get over an abiding sense of guilt that they aren't doing enough for God.

The good news of the gospel, however, is this: we are not saved according to our works, but according to the grace of God. We can never earn our salvation. It is a free gift from God. As Paul clearly taught the Romans, "If you confess with your mouth the Lord Jesus and believe in your heart that God has raised Him from the dead, you will be saved. For with the heart one believes unto righteousness, and with the mouth confession is made unto salvation" (10:9–10). No other means has been provided for men and women to be saved other than the shed blood of Jesus Christ on the cross of Calvary. The provision for your salvation, and for a total forgiveness of your sins and a change of your sin nature, has been made in full by Jesus Christ. There's nothing more you can add to it. You can only receive this free gift of God's mercy and love.

The *first* step toward removing the emotional pain of guilt in your life is to receive God's forgiveness. This means accepting Jesus Christ as your personal Savior and inviting God to cleanse your heart and create in you a new spiritual nature.

Have you come to that point in your life? If not, I invite you to pray today, "Lord, I accept what Jesus Christ did on the cross for my sake. I receive Him as my Savior today. I accept Your offer of forgiveness. I believe that You are completely cleansing me of my old sin nature and that You are creating in me a new spiritual nature. I receive the presence of the Holy Spirit into my life, and I ask You, Holy Spirit, to help me to live a life that is in complete conformity to that of Jesus Christ. It is in Jesus' name that I pray. Amen."

- *In your life, can you point to a time when you accepted Jesus Christ as your Savior and experienced a complete forgiveness for your sinful nature?*

_____

_____

What Do We Do When We Sin As Christians?

I would like to tell you that after I received Jesus Christ as my personal Savior at the age of twelve *all* feelings of guilt were completely removed from my life. That is not so, however.

The emotional baggage of pervasive guilt continued to manifest itself periodically.

This is not to say that my salvation was invalid. I have absolutely no doubt that my conversion was genuine, that my spiritual nature was changed, and that my heart was cleansed and forgiven on that day. What I had to face, however, was what all Christians have to face—that we continue to sin, to break God's commandments, and to give in to temptation, even after we are born again.

In my years of experience as a pastor, I have concluded that most Christians don't know what to do about the fact that they continue to sin after they have had a salvation experience, and they don't know what to do with these "sins." Let's take a look at what the Bible has to say about this.

First, the Bible says that after we have experienced God's free gift of grace, our *desire* for sin diminishes. Paul asked, "Shall we continue in sin that grace may abound?" He answered his own question, "Certainly not!" (Rom. 6:1–2). The desire for sin is greatly diminished upon experiencing God's forgiveness.

Second, the Bible acknowledges the fact that even after we are born again, we often err. Paul also admitted to the Romans, "I do what I don't want to do, and I don't do what I want to do." (See Rom. 7:15.) It is in those times that we must come to God, praying, "I'm struggling. I'm not doing well. I'm failing. Please forgive me and help me." Forgiveness is granted to the Christian the moment it is requested. Our *feeling* forgiven, however, may take some time.

Third, the Bible says that we grow in our understanding of God's grace (see 2 Peter 3:18). The more we become like Jesus Christ and are conformed to His will and likeness, the more we realize the awesome nature of God and how great the gulf is between God and mankind. Our salvation becomes an ever-increasing miracle to us! We have an increasing desire to guard our hearts against the temptations of the devil because our salvation is so precious to us.

Fourth, the Bible teaches that each and every time we have an awareness of our sin, we are to ask for God's forgiveness. There never is a time when we should feel that we are "beyond" God's ability to forgive us.

I have met Christians who say, "Well, I've sinned so many times since I was saved, I'm not sure if God will forgive me one more time," or "I've committed a sin even though I *knew* better. How can God forgive that?" The fact is, God forgives *all* our sin. We cannot fathom such mercy, but it is real nonetheless.

Surely if Jesus taught His disciples that they were to forgive other people up to "seventy times seven" for sins committed against them, our heavenly Father is able to forgive us that many times *and more!*

What the Word Says

What the Word Says to Me

If we confess our sins, He is   ------------------------------
faithful and just to forgive us   ------------------------------

our sins and to cleanse us from
all unrighteousness. (1 John
1:9)

Then Peter came to Him and
said, "Lord, how often shall
my brother sin against me, and
I forgive him? Up to seven
times?" Jesus said to him, "I do
not say to you, up to seven
times, but up to seventy times
seven." (Matt. 18:21–22)

For You, Lord, are good, and
ready to forgive,
And abundant in mercy to all
those who call upon You.
(Ps. 86:5)

Letting Go of Your Past

Once you have requested God's forgiveness, the next and vital step toward being free from guilt is to let go of your past.

In the course of my ministry, I have met countless people who are haunted by their sins. They have not been able to forgive themselves and let go of their past.

The Bible tells us that once we have repented of our sins, God both forgives them and forgets them (see Isa. 43:25). It is not the Lord, therefore, who reminds you of past sins that you have already confessed to Him. Rather, it is the one whom the Bible calls the "accuser of our brethren," the devil (Rev. 12:10). When you are confronted with images or memories of sins you have already confessed to God, it's time to say, "I refuse to accept these thoughts. God has already forgiven me of that. I'm letting this go right on by. Devil, you'll have no hold on my mind."

What the Word Says	What the Word Says to Me
I, even I, am He who blots out your transgressions for My own sake; And I will not remember your sins. (Isa. 43:25)	------------------------------ ------------------------------ ------------------------------ ------------------------------ ------------------------------
For as the heavens are high above the earth, So great is His mercy toward those who fear Him; As far as the east is from the west, So far has He removed our transgressions from us. As a father pities his children, So the LORD pities those who fear Him. For He knows our frame; He remembers that we are dust. (Ps. 103:11–14)	------------------------------ ------------------------------ ------------------------------ ------------------------------ ------------------------------ ------------------------------ ------------------------------ ------------------------------ ------------------------------ ------------------------------ ------------------------------ ------------------------------

Mistakes. We must always remember, also, that sins and mistakes are different from each other. A sin is a choice to do something that we know is against God's will. It is a willful act—one that is calculated, thought out, anticipated, and fully conscious. It is deliberately flying in the face of what we know is right in God's eyes.

A mistake is usually spur of the moment, unplanned, and made without forethought of consequences. A mistake is a miscalculation, an error in judgment.

We are to own up to our mistakes and learn from them. We are to make amends if we have hurt anyone in our mistakes. We are wise also to ask God to help us not to make the same mistake again.

We must *not,* however, beat ourselves up emotionally over the mistakes we make. To err is human. As long as we are alive, we are going to make mistakes.

False guilt. Let me also make a statement about false guilt. False guilt occurs when a person feels the guilt that appropriately belongs to another person. This kind of guilt is often experienced by those who are the victims of abuse or rejection. Parents of adult children who rebel against God's Word also tend to feel this guilt. The victims feel that they must have failed in some way, and thus, they have contributed to the rise of the abusive behavior, rejection, or rebellion. Therefore, they feel guilty for having caused the sin of someone else. If you are holding on to false guilt, you must let go of it. Ask the Lord to free you from all guilt that is associated with sins that aren't your own.

- *In your life, have you ever struggled with guilt over mistakes? Have you had an experience with false guilt? How has the Lord dealt with you in these cases?*

_____

_____

Guilt for Having "Missed God"

A number of people seem to feel that they have missed something that God wanted them to do—that the Lord called them to do something for Him and they failed to do it. They feel guilty as a result.

I encourage these people to ask themselves two questions. First, ask, "Was that call really of God, or was it something of my own desire?" If the call was not truly from God, God does not hold a person responsible for fulfilling it, even though he may have made a promise to do so.

Second, ask, "Did I have a direct opportunity to fulfill that call and turn away from it?" In some cases, people feel a rather vague call of God toward a particular area of service or ministry. But an opportunity has never presented itself in a concrete, specific way for a person to become involved in that area of ministry. They should feel no guilt for having failed God.

If, however, you feel that you had a specific call from God and a specific opportunity to fulfill it, but you did not, today is the day to turn to the Lord and say, "Lord, I'm sorry I disobeyed You. I ask You to forgive me. I put myself before You today. Whatever You want me to do from this point on, I'll do it." Take courage from the life of Jonah! He had a very specific call, and he turned his back on it. God gave him a second chance, and He'll give you a second chance too.

What the Word Says	What the Word Says to Me
Return, we beseech You, O	------------------------------
God of hosts;	------------------------------
Look down from heaven and	------------------------------
see,	------------------------------
And visit this vine	------------------------------
And the vineyard which Your	------------------------------
right hand has planted,	------------------------------
And the branch that You made	------------------------------
strong for Yourself . . .	------------------------------
Revive us, and we will call	------------------------------
upon Your name.	------------------------------
Restore us, O LORD God of	------------------------------
hosts;	------------------------------
Cause Your face to shine,	------------------------------
And we shall be saved!	------------------------------
(Ps. 80:14–15, 18–19)	------------------------------
Whether it is pleasing or dis-	------------------------------
pleasing, we will obey the voice	------------------------------
of the LORD our God to whom	------------------------------
we send you, that it may be	------------------------------

well with us when we obey the
voice of the LORD our God.
(Jer. 42:6)

----

* *In what ways are you feeling challenged to obey the Lord?*

_____

_____

Guilt That Arises from a False Concept of God

A pervasive feeling of guilt—not related to a specific sin, mistake, or lack of obedience—is a *feeling* that many people seem to have. I, too, have experienced this feeling in the past. This feeling has nothing to do with what a person *knows* to be true about the Scriptures and about what it means to be saved or forgiven. It is a feeling that is rooted in our perception of God.

As I shared with you earlier in this lesson, I grew up in an environment in which I believed God to be a very harsh, hard judge. I felt that I had to be perfect in order for God to accept me and love me, and since I knew I wasn't perfect, I had feelings of guilt that I had failed God and that I continued to fail Him daily.

What was wrong here was not my sinful state—that had been changed the moment I accepted Jesus as my Savior—but rather, my concept of God. It took years for me to acquire an accurate concept of God and to come to the point where I could feel genuine love flowing between God and me. I'm not talking about just saying, "I love You" to God. I'm talking about deep, affectionate, intimate feelings of love both for and from God.

If you are struggling with a false perception of God, I encourage you to take a long, hard look at the Gospels. See Jesus in action! Jesus is a perfect reflection of God the Father. He didn't do anything that was contrary to the nature and desire of His heavenly Father.

Jesus was tender with children. He extended forgiveness to sinners whom the rest of society was ready to stone to death.

He healed all the sick that were brought to Him. He loved others so much He was prepared to die for their sins so that they might live with God forever.

Your abusive parent is not the image of God . . . the teacher, coach, or other authority figure who treated you harshly is not the image of God . . . Jesus is! It is Jesus who longs to wrap His arms around you and say to you, "Come with Me to visit My Father. He can hardly wait to meet you."

God understands your frailties and weaknesses, and He loves you with a deep, abiding, unchanging love in spite of them. God's love for you is unconditional—He does not place any "ifs," "whens," or any other qualifiers on His love. Don't limit God's capacity to love. It is infinite, and it extends to you in all situations, circumstances, and conditions.

Refuse to trust your *feelings* about God that you learned or acquired from earthly examples, most of which are inaccurate. Trust, instead, the truth presented in God's Word. Base how you feel on the sure foundation of God's love as revealed by Jesus.

- *How do you feel about God? Are your feelings in line with the truth of God's Word?*

_____

_____

What the Word Says	What the Word Says to Me
[Jesus said], "He who has seen Me has seen the Father." (John 14:9)	_____ _____ _____
[Jesus said], "For God so loved the world that He gave His only begotten Son, that whoever believes in Him should not perish but have everlasting	_____ _____ _____ _____

life. For God did not send His
Son into the world to con-
demn the world, but that the
world through Him might be
saved." (John 3:16–17)

We have known and believed
the love that God has for us.
God is love, and he who abides
in love abides in God, and
God in him. (1 John 4:16)

We love Him because He first
loved us. (1 John 4:19)

You and only you know if you have a right understanding of
God and a right relationship with God. If you are not "right"
with God, you can be. The Lord stands ready at all times to
forgive you and to receive you fully into His presence. The
Lord's desire for you today is that you be free of guilt and sin.
All you need to do is to take Him up on His offer to carry the
load of your guilt and sin for you.

- *What new insights do you have into the provision of the
  Lord for all forms of guilt?*

  _____

  _____

- *In what ways are you feeling challenged in your spirit today?*

  _____

  _____

LESSON 7

STRENGTH IN TIMES OF FRUSTRATION

There was never a time when I felt God say directly to me, *I want you to preach.* But from the time I was saved, I never really thought about doing anything else. To me preaching always seemed to be what I was destined to do.

Since I came to adulthood with a heavy load of emotional baggage—low self-esteem, lots of insecurities, a lifelong feeling of loneliness—being a pastor was probably one of the least likely things I *should* have aspired to do. Being a pastor meant dealing with lots of people, and I had virtually no experience with that. It also meant being in a leadership position, and again, nothing in my background had prepared me for such a role.

In my feelings of inadequacy, I drove myself to be the most perfect pastor who had ever lived. I studied long and hard, prayed long and hard, and worked long and hard hours. Not only did I drive myself, I drove other people. I not only wanted God's approval, but also the approval of those who called me to be their pastor. I did what most perfectionists would do:

- I exerted control. I felt I had to be in control no matter what was happening.
- I was combative. No matter what was going on, I was ready to fight if somebody wanted to fight—not physically, of course, but in intellectual and spiritual arenas.
- I was critical. If a person didn't live up to my standard, I let my disapproval be known.

Not only was I wrong on all three counts, I also became constantly irritated and frustrated.

Irritation and frustration are inner events. The person who has pervasive feelings of irritation and frustration is a person who generally

- hasn't dealt with something,
- is running from something,
- hasn't identified something,
- refuses to recognize something, or
- refuses to confront his own inner anger.

Irritation and frustration are often rooted in an inability to accept the way God has created a person, a reluctance to face a problem in the past, or a refusal to confront something that the person knows is wrong and contrary to God's purposes and plan.

I have met countless people who have expressed to me that they have a deep inner frustration that never seems to leave them. I usually ask them, "Why are you striving so hard? What are you expecting to get or earn?"

- Is it a matter of pride—do you desire to be recognized?
- Is it a matter of control—are you seeking greater power?

- Is it a matter of inadequacy—do you still believe you must do more in order for God or another person to love you?

If so, I have good news for you. God couldn't possibly love you more than He loves you right now. If you are attempting to earn His approval, you already have it! God's word to you is, "Let Me do the striving on your behalf! Let Me do the work in you. Receive My love and forgiveness. Receive My help. Accept My offer and let Me do My perfecting work in you."

- *Have you had experiences with extreme or pervasive frustration in your life? What happened? Did you isolate the cause of your irritation? How did the Lord work in your life?*

_____

_____

What the Word Says	What the Word Says to Me
The LORD has appeared of old to me, saying: "Yes, I have loved you with an everlasting love; Therefore with lovingkindness I have drawn you. Again I will build you, and you shall be rebuilt." (Jer. 31:3–4)	_____ _____ _____ _____ _____ _____ _____
For by grace you have been saved through faith, and that not of yourselves; it is the gift of God, not of works, lest anyone should boast. (Eph. 2:8–9)	_____ _____ _____ _____

God-Given Frustration

There are times when a sense of irritability is not rooted in failure, inadequacy, or a desire for perfection, but rather, God seems to place in your spirit a type of restlessness. This type of frustration can be differentiated by four qualities:

1. You are not trying to conquer anybody or anything.
2. The onset of the frustration is usually quite sudden and intense, even though there seems to be no cause for it.
3. The frustration is not with anybody else but with yourself alone.
4. Once you move into the new path that God is leading you to walk, the frustration ends.

When this type of frustration manifests itself in your life, be glad! God is plowing up your soul and forcing you to confront and face a deeper part of your character. He is doing a work in you that is for your growth and, ultimately, your eternal good. Most people are familiar with Romans 8:28: "We know that all things work together for good to those who love God, to those who are the called according to His purpose." The next two verses go on to tell us God's purpose in working all things for our good: so that we might be transformed into the likeness of Jesus Christ.

> For whom He foreknew, He also predestined to be conformed to the image of His Son, that He might be the firstborn among many brethren. Moreover whom He predestined, these He also called; whom He called, these He also justified; and whom He justified, these He also glorified. (Rom. 8:29–30)

When you have a churning feeling deep inside you—a restlessness in your soul—consider the possibility that God is in the process of "justifying" you to come into conformity with the image of Christ Jesus. Face up to any sins that the Lord may reveal to you during this time. Read God's Word with renewed vigor, be alert to those verses that God may cause to leap off the page as you read them. Start *expecting* God to show you what He is leading you to do. Thank the Lord for getting you ready for His next step in your life!

- *Have you had an experience in which your frustration was God's way of moving you into a new place, position, or posture before Him?*

- *Recall an experience through which you felt the Lord was "conforming" you to the image of Christ Jesus.*

Compulsions and Obsessions

Frustration at times results in compulsions and obsessions. These frequently are related to perfectionism. Compulsions and obsessions are traps, not blessings. They drive a person to pursue something until he gains it, regardless of who may be hurt in the process or what damage may be caused.

Frustration can also lead to greed, which is a form of obsession. The more people want, the more there is to want.

If you struggle with a general feeling of frustration that you believe there's more you *should* have in your life—more recognition, more approval, more things, more appreciation—I invite you to pause for a moment and reflect about the things that you truly value in life. What would you *not* want to lose? What do you most desire to have when you are ninety years old?

Most people who identify what they truly value in life will list such things as

- a long, fruitful, and fulfilled life;
- good health;
- a loving circle of family and friends;
- the hope of eternal life; and
- inner peace and joy.

I have good news and bad news regarding these things. The bad news is that you cannot get any of these things on your own. You cannot buy them, earn them, or acquire them. The good news is that these are the very things that the Lord desires for you to have and that He will help you to experience as you trust in Him!

- *How do you feel when you are not in control of situations or cannot acquire or do the things you desire to acquire or do? What do you do with those feelings?*

_____

_____

What the Word Says	What the Word Says to Me
Trust in the LORD with all your heart, And lean not on your own understanding; In all your ways acknowledge Him, And He shall direct your paths. (Prov. 3:5–6)	_____ _____ _____ _____ _____ _____ _____ _____
[Jesus said,] "I have come that they may have life, and that they may have it more abundantly." (John 10:10)	_____ _____ _____ _____

Frustration with Other People

While a pervasive and long-standing feeling of frustration is nearly always something that resides within a person, there are also times when it is natural to feel frustration on a short-term basis. This frustration is sometimes related to the actions of another person, generally to conflicting preferences, opinions, or personality traits. At times it is related to circumstances that are beyond our control or influence.

What are we to do in those times?

The Bible teaches that we can experience a continual feeling of inner contentment *regardless of our outward circumstances.* The apostle Paul was sitting in a Roman prison, facing all kinds of persecution and ridicule from others, when he wrote, "I have learned in whatever state I am, to be content: I know how to be abased, and I know how to abound. Everywhere and in all things I have learned both to be full and to be hungry, both to abound and to suffer need" (Phil. 4:11–12).

How did Paul find inner contentment?

By focusing on the sovereignty of God rather than on the will of people.

By praising and thanking God rather than criticizing others.

By putting trust in God to deal with the future rather than continually looking at the past.

By trusting in God to make all things right rather than distrusting human ability.

It was when Paul turned his attention to Christ and away from his circumstances and detractors that he received strength. His contentment did not rest in a denial of the outside world or the facts related to his situation. His contentment flowed from his trust in Christ Jesus.

Whether your inner restlessness comes from unresolved issues in your past, is related to people or situations over which you have no control, or is a God-given restlessness intended to draw you deeper into the Lord's will, the answer to frustration comes as you trust God.

- *Recall the most frustrating experience of your life. What did you do? What was the result?*

  _____

  _____

- *Have you had an experience in which you felt God's peace filling your spirit even though you were in the midst of seeming chaos?*

  _____

  _____

What the Word Says	What the Word Says to Me
[Jesus said], "Peace I leave with you, My peace I give to you; not as the world gives do I give to you. Let not your heart be troubled, neither let it be afraid." (John 14:27)	_____ _____ _____ _____ _____ _____
Be anxious for nothing, but in everything by prayer and supplication, with thanksgiving, let your requests be made known to God; and the peace of God, which surpasses all understanding, will guard your hearts and minds through Christ Jesus. (Phil. 4:6–7)	_____ _____ _____ _____ _____ _____ _____ _____

Frustration Rooted in Impatience

Finally, there are times when our feelings of frustration are rooted simply in a hurry-up attitude. We become impatient with the timing of certain events or changes that we desire in our lives.

A restlessness in spirit can manifest itself as a tendency to run past God's will. You may know what God wants you to do, and in eagerness to get the job done, you forget that God also has a perfect timetable for accomplishing His will. Just as the Lord has a right thing for you to do, a right path in which you are to walk, and a right growth pattern for your faith, so, too, He has a right time for each step He leads you to take.

Numerous times in the Bible we find an advantage associated with "waiting on the Lord." Waiting means, in part, saying to the Lord, "Is now the time? I'm waiting until You give me the green light before I go." If you have a pattern of getting ahead of God's timing, ask yourself, "What am I looking for in life? Why do I keep running right past God's will in trying to get it? What am I in a hurry for?"

The disadvantages of getting ahead of God are evident throughout the Bible. Abraham and Sarah got ahead of God's plan in Abraham's fathering of a child through Hagar. Peter was notorious for trying to get ahead of God's plan, even to the slicing off of a man's ear in the Garden of Gethsemane. Jesus, on the other hand, never showed up too early or too late. He always arrived right on time, in keeping with what the Father was doing.

Learning to wait on God's timing is one of the hallmarks of the mature Christian life.

What the Word Says	What the Word Says to Me
Wait on the LORD;	_____
Be of good courage,	_____
And He shall strengthen your	_____
heart;	_____
Wait, I say, on the LORD!	_____
(Ps. 27:14)	_____
I will wait for You,	_____
O You his Strength;	_____

For God is my defense
My God of mercy shall come
to meet me. (Ps. 59:9–10)

Truly my soul silently waits for
God;
From Him comes my salva-
tion.
He only is my rock and my
salvation;
He is my defense;
I shall not be greatly moved.
(Ps. 62:1–2)

    The Lord doesn't catapult us into greatness; He grows us
into spiritual maturity.

    He stretches us slowly so that we don't break.

    He expands our vision slowly so that we can take in all of
the details of what He desires to accomplish.

    He causes us to grow slowly so that we stay balanced.

    The unfolding of God's plan for your life is a lifelong
process. Relax in His presence and allow Him to lead the journey and do His work in you.

    The Lord will do whatever it takes to prod us toward His
higher places. He'll make us restless with where we are if it is
time for us to move on. He'll cause us to hunger and thirst for
more of Him. He'll plant within us a desire for things we never
dreamed of desiring in our relationship with Him.

    Trust God with *all* of the circumstances, relationships, and
schedules in your life. Rest in Him. He desires to be your
strong and sure haven in all times of frustration.

What the Word Says

[Jesus said], "Come to Me, all
you who labor and are heavy

What the Word Says to Me

laden, and I will give you rest.
Take My yoke upon you and
learn from Me, for I am gentle
and lowly in heart, and you will
find rest for your souls." (Matt.
11:28–29)

You will show me the path of
life;
In Your presence is fullness of
joy;
At Your right hand are plea-
sures forevermore. (Ps. 16:11)

- *What new insights do you have into the way the Lord strengthens those who are weakened or sidetracked by frustration and irritation?*

_____

_____

- *In what ways are you feeling challenged in your spirit today?*

_____

_____

STRENGTH IN TIMES OF BURNOUT

During my years of striving for perfection and seeking approval in my ministry, I knew that I was working too hard for an impossible ideal and that I was expecting too much of myself and others. I justified my behavior, as many perfectionists do, by saying, "God made me this way." The result was that I got on a downward spiral of more and more work in an effort to get better and better and to receive more and more approval. Eventually, I crashed hard.

In 1977 I was doing two thirty-minute television programs plus the Sunday morning television program that came from the church, in addition to everything else I was doing. I noticed that instead of just being tired on Monday, which is normal for a pastor who has preached Sunday morning and Sunday night, I was tired on Tuesday . . . and then on Wednesday . . . and then all week. I went to the hospital three times that year and had all kinds of tests, and each time the doctors found nothing wrong. I'd promise to take a little break, but it was never a long enough break to really help me. And then the time came when I was so exhausted that I finally took the "orders" of my church board to take a leave of absence for several months. I felt so drained that I wondered if I'd ever regain sufficient strength to function normally. I had lots of self-doubt to go along with the exhaustion.

During the months that followed, I did some serious introspection, and I came to the conclusion that the number-one person who was driving me was *me*. Prior to that time, I likely would have said that I was doing all I was doing because I loved God. But much of what I was doing for God, I was really doing for myself. Much of my prayer life focused on what I wanted to achieve and on what I wanted to accomplish for the church. I wanted to do it all and have it all. And in the process of pursuing it all, I came to the point of being utterly exhausted physically, mentally, and emotionally.

Have you ever been in that position? Burned out and then realizing that the number-one cause of your burnout is your own unsatisfied ambition? I know many people who have been in this situation.

- *In your life, have you had an experience with burnout, a feeling of total physical, mental, and emotional exhaustion? What did you do? How did the Lord work in your life at that time?*

_____

_____

Getting Beyond the Burnout Stage

In all, I took off twelve weeks from the church during this period of burnout. A little to my surprise, I returned to find attendance up, the offering up, and the people happy. God had taken good care of His flock! It took nearly ten more months, however, for me to feel that I was fully back physically. In the course of those ten months, I learned several principles that I believe are also reflected in God's Word.

We each must learn to rest and to pace ourselves mentally, physically, and emotionally. Mental, physical, and emotional burnout are related. The first step toward being healed of burnout nearly always includes a period of prolonged rest coupled with good nutrition. When you are physically exhausted, your mind and emotions are also impacted.

Time and again, we read in the Scriptures that Jesus withdrew from His disciples and His ministry to rest and to pray. Here are just a few examples:

- "Jesus withdrew with His disciples to the sea" (Mark 3:7).
- "He Himself often withdrew into the wilderness and prayed" (Luke 5:16).
- "And when He had sent the multitudes away, He went up on the mountain by Himself to pray" (Matt. 14:23).

Jesus knew the importance of pacing Himself—of taking time for physical, mental, and emotional rest. He knew how to have "downtime."

What the Word Says	What the Word Says to Me
Remember the Sabbath day, to keep it holy. Six days you shall labor and do all your work, but the seventh day is the Sabbath of the LORD your God. In it you shall do no work: you, nor your son, nor your daughter, nor your male servant, nor your female servant, nor your cattle, nor your stranger who is within your gates. For in six days the LORD made the	------------------------------ ------------------------------ ------------------------------ ------------------------------ ------------------------------ ------------------------------ ------------------------------ ------------------------------ ------------------------------ ------------------------------ ------------------------------

heavens and the earth, the sea, _____
and all that is in them, and _____
rested the seventh day. There- _____
fore the LORD blessed the _____
Sabbath day and hallowed it. _____
(Ex. 20:8–11) _____

[Jesus said], "The Sabbath was _____
made for man, and not man _____
for the Sabbath." (Mark 2:27) _____

• *What new insight do you have into the importance of rest and pacing in your life?*

_____

_____

We must never get too busy for the "basics" of our Christian discipline. One of the clearest signs that a person has taken on too much, is involved in too many activities, or is too intensely consumed with too many matters, is the lack of maintaining these three basic Christian disciplines:

1. *Reading God's Word.* A person needs to spend time each day in God's Word. What we read becomes part of how we think and respond to life. It becomes our nature, character, attitude, and mind-set.

2. *Spending time in prayer.* A person needs to spend time every day talking to God. This is vital if a person is to have a walking-and-talking intimacy with the Lord. Spend time telling God how you feel, thank Him for the good things in your life, praise Him for what He has done, is doing, and for who He is. Share with the Lord your worries, hopes, desires, fears, and concerns. And listen for Him to speak His words of comfort, counsel, and direction.

3. *Maintaining fellowship with other believers.* Get involved in a church with those who believe God's Word the way you do.

Attend regularly. Volunteer your services in an area where you can share your talents and gifts.

The person who is too busy to attend church, too tired to pray, and too preoccupied to read God's Word is a person whose priorities are out of line and whose schedule is likely to be overbooked. Such a person is on his way to burnout.

What the Word Says	What the Word Says to Me
[Jesus said], "Therefore do not worry, saying, 'What shall we eat?' or 'What shall we drink?' or 'What shall we wear?' For after all these things the Gentiles seek. For your heavenly Father knows that you need all these things. But seek first the kingdom of God and His righteousness, and all these things shall be added to you." (Matt. 6:31–33)	_____
O God, You are my God; Early will I seek You; My soul thirsts for You; My flesh longs for You In a dry and thirsty land Where there is no water. So I have looked for You in the sanctuary, To see Your power and Your glory. Because Your lovingkindness is better than life, My lips shall praise You. . . . My soul shall be satisfied as	_____

with marrow and fatness, --------------------------------
And my mouth shall praise You --------------------------------
with joyful lips. (Ps. 63:1–3, 5) --------------------------------

Make a decision to do only what the Lord requires. Many people reach the burnout stage because they are simply trying to do too many things at the same time. We must keep in mind that God does not commit Himself to helping us do everything *we* want to do in our lives. He is committed to helping us do only things *He* wants us to do. God spends His wisdom, His energy, and His knowledge and understanding not on the fringes of what we want to do in life but on what He wants to see accomplished. Very often the Lord allows us to reach the burnout stage to teach us His lessons:

- That we are doing more than He is requiring us to do
- That we have our priorities out of order
- That we aren't putting Him first
- That we are trying to do too many good things at the same time

If you are feeling worn out today, I suggest that you back off from everything that you are doing and reappraise your life. Make a list of everything that you are doing and also identify the time and energy required for each activity. Look for trends and patterns among the activities. Do you find a balance between mental and physical activities? Is there a balance between rest and work? And finally, ask the Lord to reveal to you as you reappraise your commitments what it is that is truly important to Him. Ask Him to show you where you need to spend more time, where you need to spend less time, and which activities you might drop. About each activity on your list, ask Him, "Is this something You want me to be doing right now, to this degree and in this way?"

- *In your life, can you recall a time when you took on more commitments or responsibilities than the Lord truly required of you? What happened? What did the Lord reveal to you through that experience?*

_____

_____

What the Word Says

What the Word Says to Me

With what shall I come before
the LORD,
And bow myself before the
High God?
Shall I come before Him with
burnt offerings,
With calves a year old?
Will the LORD be pleased with
thousands of rams,
Ten thousand rivers of oil?
Shall I give my firstborn for
my transgression,
The fruit of my body for the
sin of my soul?
He has shown you, O man,
what is good;
And what does the LORD
require of you
But to do justly,
To love mercy,
And to walk humbly with your
God? (Mic. 6:6–8)

Show me Your ways, O LORD;
Teach me Your paths.

Lead me in Your truth and
teach me,
For You are the God of my
salvation;
On You I wait all the day.
(Ps. 25:4–5)

Trust God to help you trust others. One of the most positive lessons I learned in recuperating from burnout was to yield control over certain activities and responsibilities in the church to others on the church staff. I learned to trust God to give other people both the wisdom and the skill to fill the gaps, and the energy to take up the slack, in those areas of authority that I delegated.

To trust others with supervisory or administrative authority, a person must first

- be willing to share the glory or the credit for jobs done well;
- be secure, willing to let others have relationships in which the person is not a part;
- be willing to let others make mistakes occasionally rather than to dictate that no mistakes be made (which isn't possible); and
- above all, be willing to see others grow in their faith and in their ability to trust God to work on their behalf.

Who is our role model in this? Jesus Himself. Read how Jesus sent others out into ministry:

And He called the twelve to Himself, and began to send them out two by two, and gave them power over unclean spirits. He commanded them to take nothing for the journey except a staff—no bag, no bread, no copper in their money belts—but to wear sandals, and not to put on two tunics. . . . So they went out and preached that people should repent. And they cast out many demons, and anointed with oil many who were sick, and healed them. (Mark 6:7–9, 12–13)

If Jesus could trust His ministry to others, surely we can entrust some of our responsibilities to others also!

- *What new insights do you have into Mark 6:7–9, 12–13?*

  _____

  _____

- *How do you feel about the fact that the Lord has entrusted to you and other Christians today His ministry on this earth?*

  _____

  _____

- *In what ways do you feel challenged to trust others?*

  _____

  _____

The person who has a balance of rest and work; a balance of mental work and physical work; a good pace to his life; the right priorities when it comes to time spent in Bible reading, prayer, and church involvement; who does not take on more than the Lord requires of him; and who is willing to trust others and delegate authority and responsibility to them is a person who is not likely to reach a burnout stage! Such a person is on his or her way to wholeness and a feeling of fulfillment in life.

Ask the Lord which changes He desires you to make so that you might be *whole*. Success is often man's desire for himself. But wholeness—in body, mind, emotions, spirit, and relationships—is always God's desire for mankind!

Confront Your Need to Do All and Be All

Ultimately, if you are a person who feels driven to do more and more—for whatever reason or outcome—you must come to the place where you ask yourself, "Why do I have this inner drive to do more than others do?"

The answer is going to involve some deep introspection on your part. I don't know fully what drives you or any other person to succeed regardless of the cost that success demands. What I do know is that most people I have met who have this drive are feeling a lack of God's love in some area of their lives.

I also know that any time we put down our emotional baggage and allow God to invade our memories and our emotional hurts, He will invade our lives with His love.

What a wonderful feeling it is to come to the place where you feel totally accepted and loved by God! That point came fairly late for me in my life, but what a day it was! After that experience, I had no trouble feeling that God loved me. I had no trouble trusting God to be faithful in His love. I had an inner closeness with God unlike any I had experienced previously, and that closeness has grown to an ever deeper intimacy. Parts of me were healed that I didn't even know were weak or ailing!

I encourage you to come to a point of total surrender of your life, saying to God, "I give everything to You—my life, my relationships, my schedule, my activities, my successes, my weaknesses, my failures, my insecurities, my emotions, my *all*. I invite You to take over the total responsibilities for my life and to do whatever is necessary in me to heal me and to give me a deep and abiding sense of Your approval, Your love, and Your presence."

I believe God will answer that prayer from a humble heart each and every time it is prayed.

What the Word Says	What the Word Says to Me
[Jesus said], "The one who comes to Me I will by no means cast out." (John 6:37)	------------------------------ ------------------------------ ------------------------------
And Jesus called a little child to Him, set him in the midst of them, and said, "Assuredly, I say to you, unless you are converted and become as little children, you will by no means enter the kingdom of heaven. Therefore whoever humbles himself as this little child is the greatest in the kingdom of heaven." (Matt. 18:2–4)	------------------------------ ------------------------------ ------------------------------ ------------------------------ ------------------------------ ------------------------------ ------------------------------ ------------------------------ ------------------------------ ------------------------------
Humble yourselves in the sight of the Lord, and He will lift you up. (James 4:10)	------------------------------ ------------------------------ ------------------------------

- *What new insights do you have into the provision of the Lord for those who are experiencing burnout or who are on their way to burnout?*

  _____

  _____

- *In what ways are you feeling challenged in your spirit today?*

  _____

  _____

STRENGTH IN TIMES OF PERSECUTION

What is persecution? I define it as a situation that is abusive and painful, but also a situation in which you know with certainty that God intends for you to stay and for which there seems to be no human resolution. This is especially true if a person's witness for the Lord is at stake, or if the abuse and pain are being inflicted because the behaviors of a person are based on biblical standards.

I have experienced persecution in my life, and I know that persecution can be intensely hateful and emotionally draining. At one point in my life, I experienced bitter opposition and ungodly assaults for nearly three years without any relief in sight. I forged ahead with what I knew God had called me to do by sheer faith, obedience, and endurance.

During that time I became very certain about two truths related to persecution:

1. *God is faithful.* God does not abandon us to persecution; He walks through persecution with us. He never leaves us nor forsakes us. He is with us at all times, and

it is His sustaining love and presence that support us in times of persecution.

2. *God will win.* In the end, God has the victory. Whether we live or die in a time of persecution is ultimately unimportant. God's purposes *will* be accomplished on this earth, and we can either have a part in their accomplishment or fail to have a part. The righteous will prevail. God's plan will come to fruition.

You can stake your life on these truths. They can give you the strength to endure whatever persecution comes your way.

What the Word Says	What the Word Says to Me
He is the living God,	-------------------------------
And steadfast forever;	-------------------------------
His kingdom is the one which	-------------------------------
shall not be destroyed,	-------------------------------
And His dominion shall endure	-------------------------------
to the end.	-------------------------------
He delivers and rescues,	-------------------------------
And He works signs and won-	-------------------------------
ders In heaven and on earth.	-------------------------------
(Dan. 6:26–27)	-------------------------------
Who is like You, O LORD,	-------------------------------
among the gods?	-------------------------------
Who is like You, glorious in	-------------------------------
holiness,	-------------------------------
Fearful in praises, doing	-------------------------------
wonders?	-------------------------------
You stretched out Your right	-------------------------------
hand;	-------------------------------
The earth swallowed them.	-------------------------------
You in Your mercy have led forth	-------------------------------

The people whom You have
redeemed;
You have guided them in Your
strength
To Your holy habitation . . .
Till Your people pass over, O
Lord,
Till the people pass over
Whom You have purchased.
You will bring them in and
plant them
In the mountain of Your inheri-
tance,
In the place, O Lord, which
You have made
For Your own dwelling,
The sanctuary, O Lord, which
Your hands have established.
"The Lord shall reign forever
and ever." (Ex. 15:11–13,
16–18)

The eyes of the Lord are on
the righteous,
And His ears are open to their
cry.
The face of the Lord is against
those who do evil,
To cut off the remembrance of
them from the earth.
The righteous cry out, and the
Lord hears,
And delivers them out of all
their troubles.
The Lord is near to those who

have a broken heart,
And saves such as have a con-
trite spirit.
Many are the afflictions of the
righteous,
But the LORD delivers him out
of them all. (Ps. 34:15–19)

    One of the most important things you can do when perse-
cution strikes is to *remind* yourself that God is God. He is in
control of you and of all situations and circumstances. He *will*
accomplish all that He desires to accomplish. He is all-know-
ing, all-powerful, ever-present, everlasting, and always
extending an infinite, unconditional love. When persecution
comes, make your first thought, *God is in charge! He will be the
Victor!*

God Will Deal with His Enemies

    Throughout the Scriptures we find many examples of how
the Lord deals with His enemies:

- *Swiftly.* Psalm 64:7 gives us one example, "But
  God shall shoot at them with an arrow; suddenly
  they shall be wounded."
- *Decisively.* When Moses led the children of Israel
  across the Red Sea, he told them, "The Egyptians
  whom you see today, you shall see again no more
  forever. The LORD will fight for you, and you shall
  hold your peace" (Ex. 14:13–14).
- *Absolutely.* When the sons of Korah rebelled against
  the commands of the Lord, the earth literally
  opened and swallowed them up (see Num. 16).

It is a fearful and awesome thing to fight against God, to rebel against God, or to oppose God's people.

If you are doing what the Lord has commanded you to do, and you are living in righteousness before the Lord, the enemies who come to persecute you are also putting themselves into a position to be an enemy of God. God defends His people for precisely one reason: they are *His* people.

- *What new insights do you have into the way God deals with those who rebel against Him or persecute His people?*

_____

_____

How We Deal with Times of Persecution

I believe there are five vital keys to dealing with persecution.

1. *Keep your eyes on the Lord.* Unless you keep your eyes on the Lord, you are likely to find yourself feeling angry, bitter, or resentful against those who are persecuting you. Those emotions can be just as damaging as the persecution itself. Don't compound the problem. Stay focused on Jesus!

Some people consider that all forms of persecution come from the devil. In one regard, they are correct. God never instigates, authorizes, or promotes persecution. On the other hand, God does allow persecution to come our way. We see this clearly in the life of Job in the Bible. God did not authorize the devil's persecution of Job, but He did allow the devil to test him and to bring situations into his life that might well be described as abusive.

What was God's purpose in allowing this in the life of Job? One of His purposes was to win a battle against the devil. Job's faithfulness and refusal to sin were victories for God over the devil. The Lord also used the devil's persecution in Job's personal life to prepare Job for even greater revelations of Himself.

In nearly every incident of persecution I've witnessed, I

have seen God's purposes at work in much the same way. When a person remains faithful to the Lord and refuses to sin, God gains a victory over the devil—his power is thwarted, his influence is diminished. Plus, a greater strength emerges in the body of Christ, not only in the righteous victim, but in those who witness the actions of the righteous victim. The victim of persecution who continues to trust in the Lord often has much greater revelations into the Lord's nature, His purposes on this earth, and the relationship He desires to have with the person.

- *Have you ever experienced a time of persecution in which these were the outcomes?*

_____

_____

2. *Ask the Lord to sustain you and strengthen you.* The Bible has a great deal to say about those who endure all the way *through* a period of persecution to emerge victorious on the other side. Even as you pray for the Lord to remove the cause of your persecution, pray for strength to withstand the enemy of your soul until the persecution lifts.

What the Word Says	What the Word Says to Me
[Jesus said], "He who endures to the end will be saved." (Matt. 10:22)	_____ _____ _____
I have fought the good fight, I have finished the race, I have kept the faith. Finally, there is laid up for me the crown of righteousness, which the Lord, the righteous Judge, will give to me on that Day, and not to	_____ _____ _____ _____ _____ _____ _____

What the Word Says	What the Word Says to Me
me only but also to all who have loved His appearing. (2 Tim. 4:7–8)	------------------------------ ------------------------------ ------------------------------
Hold fast what you have till I come. And he who overcomes, and keeps My works until the end, to him I will give power over the nations . . . and I will give him the morning star. (Rev. 2:25–26, 28)	------------------------------ ------------------------------ ------------------------------ ------------------------------ ------------------------------ ------------------------------ ------------------------------

3. *Recognize that you are fighting a spiritual battle.* To be able to withstand persecution, you must know with certainty that the battle is the Lord's—that you are being persecuted for the cause of Christ and not simply for an error or an act of your foolishness, or stubbornness. Perhaps the most potent question you can ask is a tough one, "Who will get the glory for a victory?" If the person who is applauded for the victory is anyone other than the Lord Jesus Christ, mixed motives are in play. To God be the glory for a victory over persecutors and to no one else!

In fighting a spiritual battle, we do well to remind ourselves of Paul's words to the Ephesians:

> Be strong in the Lord and in the power of His might. Put on the whole armor of God, that you may be able to stand against the wiles of the devil. For we do not wrestle against flesh and blood, but against principalities, against powers, against the rulers of the darkness of this age, against spiritual hosts of wickedness in the heavenly places. Therefore take up the whole armor of God, that you may be able to withstand in the evil day, and having done all, to stand. Stand therefore, having

girded your waist with truth, having put on the breastplate of righteousness, and having shod your feet with the preparation of the gospel of peace; above all, taking the shield of faith with which you will be able to quench all the fiery darts of the wicked one. And take the helmet of salvation, and the sword of the Spirit, which is the word of God; praying always with all prayer and supplication in the Spirit, being watchful to this end with all perseverance and supplication for all the saints. (6:10–18)

What you arm yourself with in times of persecution is especially important.

- *Arm yourself with the truth.* Make sure you know the truth of the situation from God's perspective.
- *Arm yourself with righteousness.* Make certain that you are in right standing with God and that you are living a blameless life before your persecutors. Persecution gives you no license to sin.
- *Arm yourself with God's peace.* Make peace your goal—true reconciliation, not merely a truce.
- *Arm yourself with faith.* Keep your focus on the Lord Jesus.
- *Arm yourself with the confidence of your salvation and deliverance at God's hand.* Expect the victory to come!
- *Arm yourself with the Word of God.* Be quick to speak the Word of God in the midst of your persecution. Let God's Word do your talking for you.
- Having done all to arm yourself, *endure in prayer.* Pray for those who are persecuting you. Pray for God to move on their hearts and to save them. Pray for your fellow believers that God will strengthen them as they stand with you in your time of persecution.

- And then *persevere*. Don't give up. Don't give in. Remain solidly grounded in the Lord and *stand*.

- *What other insights do you have into Ephesians 6:10–18?*

_____

_____

4. *Continue to treat your persecutors with godly love and kindness.* Our first impulse is nearly always to respond to persecution with equal force—to retaliate, to fight, to go on the offensive even as we build a strong defense against our persecutors. The Bible presents a very different course of action to us. Jesus taught that we are to treat our persecutors with kindness—speaking well of them, praying for them, and responding to them with godly love. This is tough to do, but this is what we are commanded by the Lord to do!

Jesus also taught that we are to turn the other cheek to those who strike us, that we are to "give" in times of persecution, rather than to withdraw or to wither into silent submission. In many ways, giving is a very strong action to take in persecution. Giving and showing kindness are acts that confound and foil the attempts of persecutors. The anger and hatred felt by a persecutor can't help but be thwarted when that persecutor is faced with a loving, giving, praying victim! Ask the Lord to give you the strength to become an active *giver* in times of persecution, not only an enduring saint.

What the Word Says	What the Word Says to Me
[Jesus said], "But I say to you who hear: Love your enemies, do good to those who hate you, bless those who curse you, and pray for those who spitefully use you. To him who	_____ _____ _____ _____ _____ _____

What the Word Says	What the Word Says to Me
strikes you on the one cheek, offer the other also. And from him who takes away your cloak, do not withhold your tunic either. Give to everyone who asks of you. And from him who takes away your goods do not ask them back. And just as you want men to do to you, you also do to them likewise." (Luke 6:27–31)	----------------------------- ----------------------------- ----------------------------- ----------------------------- ----------------------------- ----------------------------- ----------------------------- ----------------------------- ----------------------------- ----------------------------- -----------------------------
[Jesus said], "But if you love those who love you, what credit is that to you? For even sinners love those who love them. And if you do good to those who do good to you, what credit is that to you? For even sinners do the same. And if you lend to those from whom you hope to receive back, what credit is that to you? For even sinners lend to sinners to receive as much back. But love your ene-mies, do good, and lend, hoping for nothing in return; and your reward will be great, and you will be sons of the Most High. For He is kind to the unthankful and evil. There	----------------------------- ----------------------------- ----------------------------- ----------------------------- ----------------------------- ----------------------------- ----------------------------- ----------------------------- ----------------------------- ----------------------------- ----------------------------- ----------------------------- ----------------------------- ----------------------------- ----------------------------- ----------------------------- ----------------------------- ----------------------------- ----------------------------- -----------------------------

fore be merciful, just as your
Father also is merciful." (Luke
6:32–36)

- *How do you feel about God's command to love your enemies and do good to them? In what practical ways might a person show love to an enemy?*

_____

_____

5. *Look for the victory.* Never lose sight of the goal, the reason you are enduring the pain and rejection you may be experiencing. Jesus taught,

> Blessed are those who are persecuted for righteousness'
> sake,
> For theirs is the kingdom of heaven.
> Blessed are you when they revile and persecute you, and
> say all kinds of evil against you falsely for My sake.
> Rejoice and be exceedingly glad, for great is your reward
> in heaven. (Matt. 5:10–12)

The kingdom of heaven is to be gained through your persecution. Not only that, but a great reward within the kingdom of heaven is yours. There's no comparison between the earthly, transient anger of persecutors and the glory of eternity. Always keep in mind that persecution is only for a season. As painful as it may be, all persecution is temporary. Eternity awaits!

Look, too, for the victory that will come in your own life. Look for your faith to be strengthened, for you to have a greater resolve to win souls, for your character to be refined, and for you to have greater and greater cause to praise God. Expect the clouds to lift and the glory of God to be revealed when your time of persecution is over!

• *What new insights do you have into the way the Lord desires to strengthen those who are experiencing persecution?*

_____

_____

• *In what ways do you feel challenged in your spirit today?*

_____

_____

LESSON 10

STRENGTH IN TIMES OF BROKENNESS

We all know what it means to be broken—to feel shattered or blown apart, as if our entire world has fallen apart. We all have had times when we didn't want to raise our head off the pillow and when we felt certain that the tears would never stop flowing. Brokenness is often accompanied by emptiness—a feeling of void that cannot be filled, sorrow that cannot be comforted, a wound for which there is no balm.

The most painful and difficult times of my life have been those times when I felt broken. I don't like pain, suffering, or feelings of brokenness any more than anybody else does. Certain circumstances in my life have *hurt*, at times so intensely that I thought I might never heal. But one of the things I have discovered through being broken is that *after* brokenness, we are very likely to experience God's greatest presence. After brokenness, our lives can be more fruitful, more purposeful, and more joyful. A genuine *blessing* can come in the wake of being broken.

One of the greatest examples of brokenness we have in the Bible is that of Peter, and perhaps the most famous scene in

Peter's life happened the night before Jesus was crucified. After Jesus was arrested in the Garden of Gethsemane, Peter followed at a distance to the place where Jesus was taken, the house of the high priest. As Peter sat in the courtyard of the high priest's house, a servant girl looked closely at him and said, "This man was with Jesus." Peter denied knowing Jesus.

A little while later someone else saw him and said, "You are one of them." Again, Peter denied the association. A while later, yet another person said, "He was with Him." Peter said, "I don't know what you're talking about." And at that moment, Peter came to the full realization that even though hours before he had bragged that he would never leave Jesus, even to the point of death, he had disowned Him in fear when questioned by a few lowly servants. Peter no doubt felt broken in that moment, shattered before God and before the mirror of his own soul.

Peter was talented and gifted in many ways. He was impulsive, strong-willed, outspoken, and strong physically. He was also self-centered. Yet Jesus chose Peter. Why? For the same reason He chooses us: Jesus sees all we *can* be. For us to become all we can be, however, requires at times that we experience a "breaking"—a sanding, a sifting, a chiseling of our souls so that we truly begin to be conformed to the likeness of Jesus Christ. That's what happened to Peter, and it's what happens to each one of us.

- *In your life, have you experienced times of brokenness? What did you do? What was the outcome?*

  _____

  _____

- *How do you feel about the concepts that we are broken in order that the Lord might conform us into the image of Christ Jesus, and that a blessing can come from brokenness?*

  _____

  _____

Three Key Aspects of the Breaking Process

I believe there are three aspects to God's breaking process in us. We see them in the life of Peter, but also in our own lives.

1. *God targets the area of our lives that needs to be broken.* Each of us has strengths and weaknesses, attitudes, habits, relationships, and desires. God knows the specific areas that need to be refashioned and brought to a point of greater maturity in us at any given point of our lives. One of the things that the Lord knew needed to be changed in Peter's life was his impetuous, volatile nature that was subject to intense faith one moment and intense fear the next. We see how the Lord dealt with this in Matthew 14.

Jesus came walking on the water to His disciples, who had been struggling against wind and stormy waters. The Lord called out to them, "Be of good cheer! It is I; do not be afraid." Peter answered by saying, "Lord, if it is You, command me to come to You on the water." And Jesus said, "Come." But then when Peter had gone out of the boat and walked on the water to Jesus, he got his eyes off Jesus and onto the wind. He was afraid and began to sink, crying out, "Lord, save me!" Jesus stretched out His hand and caught him and said, "O you of little faith, why did you doubt?" Together they got into the boat and the wind ceased (see vv. 27–31). Peter needed to be challenged, even "broken" in this area of his life so that he might not vacillate between faith and fear, but stand strong in faith after the crucifixion, resurrection, and ascension of Jesus.

The good news of the Scriptures is that God created us and He knows us—He not only knows us as we are right now, but He knows who we *can* be, what we *can* do, and what He has fashioned and formed us to do. In times of brokenness, place your trust in God that He is doing something in you for your eternal good and for the fulfillment of His plan and purpose in your life—even though you may not be able to discern that plan and purpose fully in your immediate pain. God is at work! He has not abandoned you in brokenness—rather, He is working during this time and in this situation to create in you something good.

• *In your life, can you identify an area that the Lord may be "targeting" for greater growth and maturity?*

_____

_____

What the Word Says

Before I formed you in the
womb I knew you;
Before you were born I sancti-
fied you. (Jer. 1:5)

O LORD, You have searched me
and known me.
You know my sitting down and
my rising up;
You understand my thought
afar off.
You comprehend my path and
my lying down,
And are acquainted with all
my ways.
For there is not a word on my
tongue,
But behold, O LORD, You
know it altogether.
You have hedged me behind
and before,
And laid Your hand upon me.
Such knowledge is too won-
derful for me;
It is high, I cannot attain it.
(Ps. 139:1–6)

What the Word Says to Me

----

2. *God arranges the circumstances and chooses the tools that lead to our being broken.* Why did Jesus walk on water to His disciples? In part, He was setting up the situation in which He could teach Peter and the other disciples.

God always brings about the circumstances of our breaking in two ways. At times, He engineers the situation that will cause us to confront what He desires to change in us. At other times, God will simply allow us to follow the path of sin and error that we have chosen. He will give us enough rope so we can entangle ourselves.

God also chooses the tools with which to break us—He allows us to confront the hurtful remarks or false accusations of people, erroneous negative reports, or people who attempt to manipulate us for their own purposes. He chooses the methods, sometimes even allowing our enemies to be tools in His hands.

What we must realize in times of brokenness is that God's methods and His "ways" are not always going to be readily understood by us. In fact, most of the time God's ways will confound us—He often chooses the very opposite of what *we* would choose as a tool or circumstance in which to work for our good.

What the Word Says	What the Word Says to Me
"For My thoughts are not your thoughts, Nor are your ways My ways," says the LORD.	------------------------------ ------------------------------ ------------------------------ ------------------------------
"For as the heavens are higher than the earth, So are My ways higher than your ways, And My thoughts than your thoughts.	------------------------------ ------------------------------ ------------------------------ ------------------------------ ------------------------------ ------------------------------

For as the rain comes down
and the snow from heaven,
And do not return there,
But water the earth,
And make it bring forth and
bud,
That it may give seed to the
sower
And bread to the eater,
So shall My word be that goes
forth from My mouth;
It shall not return to Me void,
But it shall accomplish what I
please,
And it shall prosper in the
thing for which I sent it."
(Isa. 55:8–11)

- *In your life, what circumstances and tools has the Lord used to bring about greater spiritual maturity in you?*

3. *God controls the amount of pressure we experience in brokenness.* God sets limits on our brokenness—limits that cover both how long the brokenness continues and the amount of pain and suffering we experience. God limits the amount of hurting He allows us to do.

What might we do to hasten the end of a period of brokenness?

First, brokenness ends when we yield to God in submission. The moment we surrender completely to God, God begins to reverse the circumstances related to our brokenness and to remove the tools that He has used in the breaking process.

Second, brokenness ends when it reaches such an intensity that it will damage God's purpose for your life. God will not allow you to be broken or shattered to the point where you cannot engage in the supernatural ministry He has prepared for you. His purpose is to train you, refashion you, mold you, conform you to Christ's image—not to destroy you.

When you begin to experience a time of brokenness, yield quickly to the Lord! Ask Him to reveal to you what He is seeking to accomplish or change in your life and become willing to do what God is asking, change what God is seeking to change, or embark on what God is calling you to do.

Just as Jesus prayed in the Garden of Gethsemane, we must reach the point where we say, "Not my will, but Your will, God."

What the Word Says	What the Word Says to Me
But as for me, my prayer is to You,	_____
O LORD, in the acceptable time;	_____
O God, in the multitude of Your mercy,	_____
Hear me in the truth of Your salvation.	_____
Deliver me out of the mire, And let me not sink;	_____
Let me be delivered from those who hate me,	_____
And out of the deep waters.	_____
Let not the floodwater over-flow me,	_____
Nor let the deep swallow me up;	_____
And let not the pit shut its	_____

mouth on me.
Hear me, O LORD, for Your
lovingkindness is good;
Turn to me according to the
multitude of Your tender mercies. (Ps. 69:13–16)

Cause me to know the way in
which I should walk,
For I lift up my soul to You.
(Ps. 143:8)

Restoration After Brokenness

Once we yield ourselves fully to the goals that the Lord is seeking to accomplish in our lives, the Lord often reveals Himself to us in extremely loving and tender ways. This happened in the life of Peter.

It took Peter three years to come to the place where he was willing to say to Jesus, "Yes, I'll be and do what You want me to be and do. I give up all control to You. I surrender my all—all that I am, all that I have, all that I will ever be."

After the crucifixion of Jesus, Peter returned to fishing. Jesus found him there by the seashore one morning, and He said to him, "Peter, do you love Me?"

Three times Jesus asked this question, and three times Peter said, "Lord, You know I do!"

Jesus fully restored Peter to a relationship with Himself. He forgave him fully for his denial: three times, Peter denied knowing Jesus, and three times, Peter had the opportunity to affirm his love for the Lord. And then, Jesus gave Peter something very specific to do: to feed and care for "the sheep"—the followers of Jesus who were in need of a leader. Peter finally yielded fully to what it was that the Lord desired for him. The Lord gave him a supernatural ministry objective, one that was realized in a powerful way beginning on the day of Pentecost. (See Peter's powerful sermon in Acts 2.)

The Lord's purpose in brokenness may have many facets to it, but one thing will always result: a greater opportunity for ministry to others. In the aftermath of your pain, discouragement, and heartache, the Lord will give you opportunities to minister to others who are going through a similar experience. Your time of brokenness prepares you for a time of greater fruitfulness in your ministry and your witness to the love and power of Christ Jesus.

Brokenness is a pruning process. Jesus taught, "Every branch in Me that does not bear fruit He takes away; and every branch that bears fruit He prunes, that it may bear more fruit" (John 15:2). If you truly are going to be fruitful in the Lord's kingdom, you *will* experience a pruning process, a refining process. The end result will be not only for your good, but for the good of others and for the expansion of the Lord's kingdom.

What the Word Says	What the Word Says to Me
I . . . Will refine them as silver is refined, And test them as gold is tested. They will call on My name, And I will answer them. I will say, "This is My people"; And each one will say, "The LORD is my God." (Zech. 13:9)	_____ _____ _____ _____ _____ _____ _____ _____ _____
But who can endure the day of His coming? And who can stand when He appears? For He is like a refiner's fire	_____ _____ _____ _____

And like launderers' soap.
He will sit as a refiner and a
purifier of silver;
He will purify the sons of Levi,
And purge them as gold and
silver,
That they may offer to the
LORD
An offering in righteousness.
(Mal. 3:2–3)

- *Recall a time of brokenness in your life. In what ways are you now better prepared to minister to others who are experiencing a similar period in their lives?*

_____

_____

- *In what ways did a period of brokenness in your life purify you or "refine" you in your character and your spiritual nature?*

_____

_____

- *How do you feel about the result of brokenness being greater ability to bear spiritual fruit?*

_____

_____

The Blessings from Brokenness

At least five blessings come from our being broken before the Lord:

1. *We understand God better.* We come into a greater understanding of the absolutes of God—that His commandments are exact, His promises are sure, His methods and timetable are His own, His provision is complete. We understand more

fully the Scriptures. We come to a greater understanding of all of God's many attributes.

2. *We understand ourselves better.* When we are broken, we understand more about our own inner motivations, desires, and weaknesses. Very often, we experience an opportunity to ask God's forgiveness in areas of life that we had not thought to confront or to explore. We have an opportunity to be freed from confusion about our own past. We have an opportunity to experience God's healing of very old emotional wounds.

3. *We have increased compassion for others.* Usually when a person gains new insight into himself through an experience of brokenness, that person emerges from the experience with a greater empathy for others and a greater compassion for those who are hurting or struggling in their lives. Brokenness makes us less critical and judgmental.

4. *We have a greater enthusiasm for life.* When we come to the end of ourselves and stand on the brink of God's unlimited, unfathomable, unconditional love, we find that we have a greater appreciation for all of God's gifts to us. Life takes on a new zest! We often find that we are more creative and more willing to express ourselves. We have a greater ability to enjoy those things that amount to good, clean, pure *fun.*

5. *We have an increased awareness of God's presence.* God is with us always, but brokenness often makes us more keenly aware of His presence and more sensitive to His desires. In feeling God's presence with us, we have a greater feeling of security.

Is brokenness worth the pain and struggle? With blessings such as these—and an increased fruitfulness in our ministry—we can say with joy as we look back on a period of brokenness, "I am grateful for all that I've been through." The key, however, is in turning to the Lord in our brokenness. Those who turn to any other person or thing, or seek to escape or deny their brokenness, find themselves in a position to experience only more of the same—and often even greater pain, discouragement, or despair. Trust God, and God alone, to do *His* work in you in times when you feel shattered, broken, or as if your world is falling apart. Allow Him to put you back together in *His* way, in *His* timing, and always, for *His* purposes.

- *Recall a period of brokenness in your life. In what ways did you experience these blessings as you trusted in God to do His work in your life and as you emerged from your experience of brokenness?*

  _____

  _____

- *What new insights do you have into the strength the Lord offers to those who are experiencing brokenness?*

  _____

  _____

- *In what ways are you feeling challenged in your spirit today?*

  _____

  _____

CONCLUSION

FROM STRENGTH TO STRENGTH

The Lord is never satisfied with the level of spiritual maturity that we have reached in our lives. He is always seeking to help us grow *more and more* into the full likeness of Jesus Christ. This, of course, is a lifelong process. None of us will ever arrive fully at that point. But, oh, the joy we can experience as we draw closer and closer to the Lord and develop an increasingly intimate relationship with our heavenly Father!

Read these wonderful words from the psalmist and make them your own hope:

> *Blessed is the man whose strength is in You,*
> *Whose heart is set on pilgrimage . . .*
> *They go from strength to strength;*
> *Every one of them appears before God in Zion.*
> *(Ps. 84:5, 7)*

Every person I know goes through periods of loneliness, fear, abuse, criticism, guilt, frustration, burnout, persecution, and brokenness—to some degree, in some way, at some time. The call of God in these periods is this: "Trust in Me! Allow Me to be your Source of Strength, your Provider, your Teacher, your Guide, your Comforter, your Savior, your Deliverer, your Healer, your Friend!"

The Lord wants to be so much *more* to you than you have ever dreamed. He wants to be the One on whom you rely completely, the One to whom you turn immediately in all situations and circumstances, and the One in whom you place your total confidence for all eternity.

Developing inner strength is ultimately a matter of developing a more intimate relationship with the One who created you, loves you, and desires to have daily fellowship with you. To develop inner strength, develop your relationship with your heavenly Father. He will give you the courage, joy, and love that you desire!